CONF
DEVE
CW00400351

About the series

Development Matters is a series of comprehensive but concise introductions to the key issues in development studies. It offers politically engaged and challenging critiques while demonstrating academic and conceptual rigour to provide readers with critical, reflexive and challenging explorations of the pressing concerns in development. With carefully designed features, such as explanatory text boxes, glossaries and recommended reading, the series provides the reader with accessible guides to development studies.

Series editor: Helen Yanacopulos

About the author

Eleanor O' Gorman lives in Cambridge and works as an independent strategist and researcher on international development, conflict and security issues. She advises, among others, the UN, the UK Government, the Government of Ireland, the European Commission, and the Organisation for Economic Co-operation and Development. Eleanor has extensive field experience in conflict-affected countries, including the Democratic Republic of Congo, Liberia, Sri Lanka and Timor Leste. With a PhD in Social and Political Sciences from the University of Cambridge, she has previously lectured at the University of East Anglia on development studies, and held the post of senior policy adviser with the UNDP (United Nations Development Programme) in New York and Brussels. Eleanor is currently Senior Associate at the Gender Studies Centre and Research Associate at the Department of Politics and International Studies at the University of Cambridge and serves as an expert on international panels and forums.

CONFLICT AND DEVELOPMENT

DEVELOPMENT **MATTERS**

ELEANOR O' GORMAN

Zed Books
London & New York

Conflict and Development was first published in 2011 by Zed Books Ltd, 7 Cynthia Street, London N1 9JF, UK and Room 400, 175 Fifth Avenue, New York, NY 10010, USA

www.zedbooks.co.uk

Designed and typeset in Sabon by Kate Kirkwood
Index by Mike Kirkwood
Cover designed by Rogue Four Design

Printed and bound in Great Britain by
CPI Antony Rowe, Chippenham and Eastbourne

Distributed in the USA exclusively by Palgrave Macmillan, a division of St Martin's Press, LLC, 175 Fifth Avenue, New York, NY 10010, USA

A catalogue record for this book is available from the British Library.
Library of Congress Cataloging in Publication Data available

ISBN 978 1 84813 574 1 hb
ISBN 978 1 84813 575 8 pb

Contents

Acknowledgements   vi

Acronyms   viii

1 International Conflict and Development   1
   in the Twenty-First Century: an Overview

2 Greed, Grievance and Poverty: 20
   the Politics of Analysing Conflict

3 Using Conflict Analysis Frameworks   44

4 The Aid Policies and Architecture of   66
   International Conflict and Development

5 Women, Peace and Security: the Gendering   92
   of International Conflict and Development

6 Fragile States and the Limits of   115
   Peacebuilding and Statebuilding

Notes   137

Bibliography   147

Index   171

Acknowledgements

This book is born of many years spent working across the academic, policy and practical divides of war and development. It owes much to the many people I have worked with, met, and been inspired by in many parts of the world. Often in modest and unsung ways, they have sought to change the world of people caught up in violent conflict and its aftermath. I am grateful to the editor of this series, Helen Yanacopulos, for encouraging me finally to put pen to paper and analyse some of the learning and dilemmas of this work. The shortcomings of this outcome are entirely my own. I would also like to thank Tamsine O'Riordan and Jakob Horstmann of Zed Books for their editorial guidance and advice, and Kate and Mike Kirkwood for their support in the production process. I thank the Palgrave Macmillan rights department for its kind permission to reprint the diagram found in Chapter 3 from Chris Mitchell's *The Structure of International Conflict*.

I am grateful to both the Centre for Gender Studies and the Department of Politics and International Studies at the University of Cambridge for the intellectual home they provide and the opportunity to bridge academic and policy communities. I would like to thank Murray Edwards College (formerly New Hall), Cambridge, for providing a supportive and collegial setting that dates back to my PhD days there. I owe a particular debt of gratitude to postgraduate students at the School of Development Studies, University of East Anglia, Norwich who took my experimental module on 'Conflict, Intervention and Development' during 1994–7, when my thinking on these issues began to emerge. It has been a gratifying and somewhat surreal experience to meet some of them in unlikely places around the world!

The following colleagues and friends have encouraged and supported me through the process of this book in different ways, and I want them to know they are deeply appreciated: Piera Beretta, Mónica Brito Vieira, Jude Browne, Stephen Chan, Deirdre Collings, Anne Considine, Barbara Cullinane, Veronica Foody, Ameerah Haq, Pierre Harzé, Chris Hill, Stine Jacobsen, Maria Mc Loughlin, Leo Mellor, Jonathan Moore, Mike MccGwire, Robert Patterson, Rafal Rohozinski, Isabella Rossa, Uli Spies Barnes, Elsa Strietman, Sophie Turenne, Jim Whitman and Helen Yanacopulos. I want to make special mention of the late Keith Webb, who was an inspiring teacher and thinker on the nature and impact of violent conflict, and takes some of the blame for setting me on my present path after completing an MA in International Conflict Analysis at the University of Kent at Canterbury. A special word of thanks goes to my wonderful sister, Mae O' Gorman Clarke, who formatted the chapters, struggled with text boxes and sat with me side by side in the final days of the manuscript. I also want to thank my father John and brother Ger for their encouragement in the process of writing this book. I am grateful to my extended family, near and far, for their unstinting support. As in all life projects, there are so many influences. I apologise if I have left someone out of this inevitably limited list.

Acronyms

ACCORD	African Centre for the Constructive Resolution of Disputes
ACORD	Agency for Cooperation and Research in Development
ALNAP	Active Learning Network for Accountability and Performance in Humanitarian Assistance
AMISOM	African Union Mission in Somalia
AU	African Union
AVR	armed violence reduction
CHASE	Conflict, Humanitarian and Security Department (DFID)
CHD	Centre for Humanitarian Dialogue
CSCW	Centre for the Study of Civil War at PRIO
CSO	civil society organisation
DDR	disarmament, demobilisation and reintegration
DFID	UK Department for International Development
DRC	Democratic Republic of Congo
ECOWAS	Economic Community of West African States
FCO	Foreign and Commonwealth Office
FEWER	Forum on Early Warning and Early Response
G8	Group of 8 (Canada, France, Germany, Italy, Japan, Russia, UK, US)
GHA	global humanitarian assistance
GNI	gross national income
GPI	Global Peace Index

GTZ/BMZ	(German) Association for Technical Cooperation/Federal Ministry for Economic Cooperation and Development
HIPC	heavily indebted poor country
HSRP	Human Security Research Project
IANSA	International Action Network on Small Arms
ICG	International Crisis Group
ICRC	International Committee of the Red Cross
IDMC	Internal Displacement Monitoring Centre
IDPs	internally displaced person(s)
IDRC	International Development Research Centre
ILO	International Labour Organisation
INCAF	International Network on Conflict and Fragility (at the OECD DAC)
INGO	international non-governmental organisation
IR	International Relations
ISAF	International Security Assistance Force in Afghanistan
LDC	least-developed country
MDGs	Millennium Development Goals
MoD	Ministry of Defence
NATO	North Atlantic Treaty Organisation
NGO	non-governmental organisation
ODA	Official Development Assistance
ODI	Overseas Development Institute
OECD DAC	Organisation for Economic Co-operation and Development, Development Assistance Committee
PCIA	peace and conflict impact assessment
PLO	Palestine Liberation Organisation
PRIO	Peace Research Institute Oslo, Norway
R2P	responsibility to protect
SALW	small arms and light weapons
SCA	strategic conflict assessment

SCR	Security Council Resolution (UN)
SEA	sexual exploitation and abuse
SGBV	sexual and gender-based violence
SIDA	Swedish International Development Agency
SIPRI	Stockholm International Peace Research Institute
SRSG	Special Representative of the Secretary-General (UN)
SSR	security sector reform
UCDP	Uppsala Conflict Data Project
UN	United Nations
UNAMID	African Union/ United Nations Hybrid Operation in Darfur
UNDP	United Nations Development Programme
UN DPKO	United Nations Department of Peacekeeping Operations
UNIFEM	United Nations Development Fund for Women
UN OCHA	United Nations Office for the Coordination of Humanitarian Affairs
UNTAET	United Nations Transitional Administration in East Timor
UPSP	Uppsala Conflict Data Project
USAID	United States Agency for International Development
WANEP	West Africa Network for Peace
WB	World Bank
WIPNET	Women in Peacebuilding Programme

1 | International Conflict and Development in the Twenty-First Century: an Overview

The new breed of intra-state conflicts has certain charac-teristics that present United Nations peacekeepers with challenges not encountered since the Congo operation of the early 1960s. They are usually fought not only by regular armies but also by militias and armed civilians with little discipline and with ill-defined chains of command. They are often guerrilla wars without clear front lines. Civilians are the main victims and often the main targets. Humanitarian emergencies are commonplace and the combatant author-ities, in so far as they can be called authorities, lack the capacity to cope with them. The number of refugees regis-tered ... has increased.... The number of internally displaced persons has increased even more dramatically. Another feature of such conflicts is the collapse of state institutions, especially the police and judiciary, with resulting paralysis of governance, a breakdown of law and order, and general banditry and chaos. Not only are the functions of govern-ment suspended, its assets are destroyed or looted and experienced officials are killed or flee the country.... It means that international intervention must extend beyond military and humanitarian tasks and must include the pro-motion of national reconciliation and the re-establishment of effective government. (Secretary-General Boutros Boutros-Ghali, on the Fiftieth Anniversary of the United Nations in 1995)

Introduction

The aim of this book is to map out the thinking and practices that are redefining contemporary responses to violent conflict in the Global South[1] and generating new possibilities and dilemmas for the moral, legitimate and practical role of international development assistance in the twenty-first century. The book focuses on the post-Cold War period since 1989 and traces the emergence and rapid expansion of a field of endeavour called Conflict and Development that seeks to enable international aid policies and programmes to better prevent, respond to, and even transform the occurrence of war and large-scale violent conflict. It explores, from the viewpoints of theory, policy and practice, a set of core themes that have both driven and arisen from this agenda over the past two decades. They provide a critical intro-duction to major aspects of the relationship between contem-porary international conflict and development through the following chapters:

- understanding violent conflict and its relationship with poverty and development (Chapter 2);

- designing and using conflict analysis as a tool for develop-ment (Chapter 3);

- the evolving international aid architecture – policies and organisations, including competing ideas of security – that shapes the conflict and development agenda (Chapter 4);

- the political momentum surrounding women, peace and security and its implications for gendered understandings of conflict, violence and development (Chapter 5);

- the current dominance of the peacebuilding/statebuilding axis and to what extent it may indicate the overreach of develop-ment policies and programmes in conflict zones (Chapter 6).

This agenda of conflict and development has brought forth new dilemmas: how can soldiers, diplomats and aid workers work together in conflict situations? How to classify development assistance in complex situations and not squeeze traditional poverty reduction programmes? Is aid always compromised in war-affected situations? How do we measure success? Critical engagement with the idea of 'new wars' and the policy and practices of the 'liberal peace' and its institutional reach run through the book and are re-evaluated in the final chapter on peacebuilding and statebuilding to focus on current dilemmas.

New wars and liberal peace

The post-Cold War world opened up the possibility of new international responses to a range of peace, security and development issues ranging from civil wars, human rights abuses, proliferation of small arms and landmines, through to natural resource conflicts, environmental degradation and HIV/Aids. This moment of optimism was captured in 'An Agenda for Peace' by UN Secretary-General Boutros Boutros-Ghali in 1992, in which he outlined an approach of preventive diplomacy, peacemaking, peacekeeping and peacebuilding that would expand the interventions of the UN in conflicts where Cold War vetoes by Security Council members had hitherto paralysed action.[2] Little cited or commented upon is the accompanying 'Agenda for Development' of 1995 and its vision of new possibilities for the relationship between peace, security and development. It called for development as peacebuilding based on the premise that 'only sustained efforts to resolve underlying socio-economic, cultural and humanitarian problems can place an achieved peace on a durable foundation' (UN 1995). From 1989, the international community became involved in new types of international humanitarian and peacekeeping operations where there was no peace to keep, a humanitarian imperative to act and yet an incapacity to enforce an end of hostilities (Bosnia and Herzegovina, Somalia). There was also an increasingly civilian dimension to peacekeeping operations, where peace agreements were negotiated and supported in implementation in areas such as organising elections, handling return of refugees, coordinating reconstruction, monitoring human rights, de-mining, policing, and overseeing transitional administration (Namibia, Angola, Mozambique, Cambodia, El Salvador, Kosovo and Timor-Leste). Peacekeepers also acquired a further role in protecting humanitarian convoys and operations to prevent looting and attacks. Within this new generation of peacebuilding and conflict prevention responses, boundaries among military, humanitarian, political/diplomatic and development approaches have been challenged and transformed.

The period of 1990–2010 brings us through the troubled and failed humanitarian interventions of the early 1990s in Somalia, Rwanda and Bosnia to the statebuilding ambitions of armed interventions in Afghanistan and Iraq. Two particular political trends define the understanding of and response to international conflict, and inform the themes taken up in this book:

1. The changing nature of conflict from inter-state to intra-state, with an emphasis on resurgent nationalism, ethnic conflict, civil wars, and the financing of conflict – including the growth of regional and global networks of arms, minerals and organized crime. This trend revolves around debates on the nature of 'new wars' in terms of the dynamics of globalisation and localisation in intra-state wars and the emergence of the 'liberal peace thesis' as a guide to international responses informing increasingly comprehensive peace operations spanning peacekeeping, diplomatic, humanitarian, rule of law and development interventions. The

norms of 'humanitarian intervention' and the 'responsibility to protect' as guides to action are part of these debates.

2. In the last decade the changing global context of violent conflict has been altered again by concerns of terrorism and so-called failed or fragile states, whereby underdevelopment itself becomes a threat to international security. This is driving new variations of the relationship between military security and development – captured by current preoccupations with stabilisation and the peacebuilding/statebuilding nexus as the template for preventing and recovering from contemporary violent conflict. In Iraq and Afghanistan this nexus potentially extends into areas of counterinsurgency and anti-terrorist objectives.

The 'new wars' debate shaped the understanding of violent conflicts that erupted in the early 1990s and brought with them new understandings of the local and global, unfettered by the superpower struggles of the Cold War period. Mary Kaldor (2006 [1999]: 8), credited with coining the phrase, describes such wars as 'a mixture of war, crime and human rights violations'. Others interpret them as inherently irrational, driven by ethnic rivalries and nationalist fervour giving rise to a 'new barbarism' (Kaplan 1993; 1994). Kaldor, along with Mark Duffield, argues for the formative role of globalisation in shaping the form and nature of new intrastate wars linked into global economic and political processes and transformations. This legacy of globalisation includes the changing world economy in terms of the rise of private sector actors in developing countries and the deregulation of markets, the growing reach and speed of technology and communications, and the emergence of transnational political networks and organisations (Kaldor 2006 [1999]: 4–10; Duffield 2001: 2–9). The new wars were typified by the rise of intra-state as opposed to inter-state conflicts and by extremely violent guerrilla and counterinsurgency clashes in which non-state actors such as militias and armed groups challenged government authority or filled a vacuum of governance, operating across borders in many cases. Furthermore, these wars were underpinned by economic incentives to ensure supplies and access to arms and resources. Thus war economies were not simply serving political ends; instead, economic gain and disruption, linked into regional and global supply chains (for example, arms, drugs, and diamonds), became ends in themselves – fuelling further violence.

Some critics argue that the differences between new and old wars have been overstated and point to the history of 'low intensity conflict', guerrilla warfare and counterinsurgency before 1990 (Fearon and Laitin 2003; Kalyvas 2001). Others argue that the evidence of greater atrocity and ferocity does not stand up to statistical or historical analysis, and point instead to declining civilian deaths since the end of the Cold War (Melander et al. 2009; Newman 2004). Even if there is disagreement on the label of 'new', there is some consensus on the trends of wars emerging in the aftermath of the bipolar Cold War order. These include: the implication and targeting of civilians with brutal violence; the availability and use of small arms and light weapons carried by ever-younger armies that are well organised and dispersed over wide areas (the notorious Lord's Resistance Army rebel group can lay claim to conflict in the Democratic Republic of Congo, Central African Republic and Southern Sudan, having originated and being active in northern Uganda until 2005); the forced recruitment of child soldiers; and the financing of war through criminal activity and networks – whether smuggling petrol and weapons in the Balkans, 'taxing' mineral resources in the Democratic Republic of Congo, or drug trading in Colombia.

Alongside the debates on new wars came the framing of international responses to them; as outlined above, the nature of international responses expanded rapidly at policy and operational levels. These developments have often been framed as the advance of 'liberal peace', exemplified by Michael Doyle (1983a; 1983b), a political theorist and former UN adviser who builds on Immanuel Kant's liberal internationalism found in *Perpetual Peace* (1795 [1939]) to propose that an inherent peacefulness of relations among a growing set of liberal states (defined by individual rights, market economy, private property, state sovereignty and democratic representative government) since the late eighteenth century is indicative of a positive potential for liberal peace to be advanced and encouraged in the foreign policy of liberal states with regard to non-liberal states. These relations have been at best mixed, with a failure to hold to liberal principles in the foreign policy of liberal states – so that dictators are supported, client states are created (reflecting the Cold War context) and a penchant for external intervention is evident, despite the liberal dictum of non-intervention among liberal states. Human rights policy and international trade have been two aspects of this, but need to be improved and added to – according to Doyle – in meeting the strategic interests of liberal states and expanding the liberal peace zone to non-liberal states. For social democratic liberals[3] in particular, international aid is an important dimension of foreign policy: it is seen as helping countries to provide the basic human needs of their people while growing the market economy and political participation as routes to growth and development. Also, aid incorporates humanitarian obligations to assist poorer people and 'limited obligations of international justice'. Such ideas of the liberal peace are seen to underpin the institutional development of increasingly complex and technical interventions in peacebuilding internationally, and more precisely in the process of statebuilding to enable functioning post-conflict states to provide stability and security as well as public services to their citizens.

This narrative of change in the international order to respond to more complex and localised wars of the past 20 years – liberal peace as a counter to new wars – has come under heavy attack. Some critics emphasise that the ideology driving this emergence of security and development interventions is part of a neo-liberal world order linking globalisation, capitalism and democracy within the broad assumption of a post-Cold War 'liberal peace' (Duffield 2001; Paris 2002). Others point to the predominant role of the economic interests of developed countries in international development concerns and involvement in conflicts in the Global South (Cooper 2005; Pugh 2005). Yet others see the focus on statebuilding as reifying the state at the expense of civil society and identity politics (Richmond 2008a). Critical arguments extend to the negative role of international development and peace interventions – whether stemming from the UN, bilateral aid,[4] or NGOs – in contributing to the dominance of the neo-liberal order; in this scenario, the human face of aid disguises the global interests and drivers for insecurity that lie behind it. These polarised perspectives reveal the current state of tension and self-critical reflection that is experienced by development actors and concerned observers on the role of development in conflict situations in the twenty-first century. An overview of recent facts and figures underscores how the interconnections of violent conflict and development persist in interesting ways that beg the question: what can and should be rescued from current understanding of and responses to international conflict?

Disciplinary debates: academic roots of conflict and development

The relationship between violent conflict, peace and development has academic roots in a range of disciplines, not least in conflict

Conflict and development: facts and figures[5]

1 Since 1989 the trend in armed conflict has moved decisively from inter-state conflict (between sovereign states) to intra-state conflicts (within state borders) with often regional and international dynamics and drivers of violence:

- in 2009 there were 36 recorded armed conflicts, all of them intra-state;
- six of these are 'major armed conflicts' or 'wars', i.e., measuring more than 1,000 battle-related deaths in one year – Sri Lanka, Pakistan, Afghanistan, Iraq, Rwanda and Somalia;
- seven of the conflicts have become internationalised, i.e., involving troops from other states – Afghanistan, Algeria, Uganda (involved in fighting in the Democratic Republic of Congo, southern Sudan and the Central African Republic), USA (leading a coalition fighting Al-Qaida), Iraq, Rwanda and Somalia (SIPRI 2010; Harbom and Wallensteen 2010).

2 During 1990–2010 there have been declining numbers of armed conflicts and people killed as a result of armed conflict:

- UCDP (see note 5) estimates that the number of state-based armed conflicts in the post-Cold War period peaked in the early 1990s at 50, and has been steadily declining until about 2006 at 32; it has stabilised at around 35 for the past few years;
- the Human Security Report Project (2005; 2006) estimates that non-state-based conflicts have declined from 34 to 25 during 2002–5, though sub-Saharan Africa remains the main focus of such wars, particularly Somalia, Nigeria, Côte d'Ivoire, Ethiopia and Sudan;
- the HSRP also estimates that state-based conflict fatalities have fallen from 15,722 in 2002 to 12,039 in 2005; non-state-based conflict fatalities have fallen from 7,014 in 2002 to 2,046 in 2005.

Continued

3 Global aid contributions have increased steadily rather than dramatically over the past 20 years and global commitments such as reaching ODA levels of 0.7 per cent of national income by 2015 are fading fast. In 2008, global humanitarian assistance was US$7 billion;[6] global ODA for 2009 was US$119.6 billion[7] (ALNAP 2010; GHA 2010; OECD DAC, 2010b; 2009a).

4 There are some 27.1 million internally displaced persons (IDPs), scattered within their own countries by violent conflict; Sudan, Colombia, Iraq, the Democratic Republic of Congo and Somalia face significantly high populations of IDPs, and Africa is the region most affected with 11.6m IDPs (IDMC 2010).

5 In eastern Democratic Republic of the Congo, at least 200,000 cases of sexual violence have been recorded since 1996 (UN 2009a).

6 US$4.8 trillion is the estimated annual loss of global income to violence – or, in more positive terms, a potential (forfeited) 'peace dividend' (GPI 2009).

7 Twenty-two of the 34 countries most likely to fall short of the Millennium Development Goals (MDGs) by 2015 are in or emerging from conflict (UN Millennium Project 2005: 183); seven of the ten lowest-ranking countries in the 2009 UN Human Development Index are in or emerging from conflict (UNDP 2009).

8 There are currently 15 UN-mandated peace operations worldwide, including Afghanistan, Democratic Republic of Congo, Sudan, Liberia and Timor-Leste; the costs of UN peacekeeping for 2009/10 are US$7.9 billion, equivalent to 0.5 per cent of global military spending (estimated at US$1.464 trillion) (UN DPKO 2010).

9 There are an additional ten peacebuilding offices and political missions under UN auspices, including Iraq, Nepal and Somalia.

10 The World Development Report of the World Bank for 2011 focuses on the interrelationship of conflict, security and development.

and peace studies, strategic/security studies and development studies itself. All of these disciplinary (or more accurately multi-disciplinary) strands of contemporary social sciences are seen to some extent in tense complementarity with the growth of the field of International Relations (IR). Development Studies and International Relations in particular are both multi- and sometimes inter-disciplinary fields that include economics, politics, law, anthropology, philosophy and even theology and religious studies. Yet the two disciplines take quite distinctive approaches to the relationship between international conflict, peace and development. Development Studies is often the poor relation of IR where, notwithstanding critical schools of thought, state-centric and military security themes remain dominant organising principles. There have been attempts to bring together development studies and peace and conflict themes. There has also been a proliferation of new courses and research on conflict-related themes for development (Barnett 2008; Duffield 2001; Hettne 1983; Yanacopulos and Hanlon 2006; Paris 2004). However, these themes and efforts remain somewhat fragmented, and Development Studies as a discipline has yet to come to terms fully with war and peace as central concerns of theory and practice in shaping the discipline in the way poverty and economics do.

The relationship between conflict and development is contested in terms of worldview, assumptions about human nature and society, and intended outcomes for peace and security that underpin various policies and approaches. A persistent debate is what causes large-scale violent conflict – and what kind of peace can we reasonably achieve and expect, and therefore what means do we use to achieve peace and security? This debate reflects the classic paradigms of International Relations – realism/conservatism, idealism/liberalism, and structuralism (Marxism and neo-Marxism) – and the schools of thought in development studies – most notably, the modernisation and *dependencia* schools.[8] Further questions are raised about the role of contemporary development itself, as theory and practice, in causing violence and conflict or as a pathway for peace (Barnett 2008; Hettne 1983). Traditional security studies/strategic studies have focused on the state as the centre of international actions and worked within the realist paradigm in viewing state interests in an international system of states as the basis for engagement and action. More recent critical international studies, reflecting the wider post-structuralist turn in the social sciences, have engaged more people-centred rather than state-centred notions of security.[9] Such is the impact of these critical trends that recent surveys of the field of security studies expand their focus to take on feminist, environmental and other critiques, and even take peace and conflict studies as part of the widened field. The emergence of peace studies and its close relation to conflict studies as sub-fields in the post-Second World War era has impacted directly on ideas and frameworks for considering the processes and dynamics of violent conflict as well as active support to conflict resolution and peacebuilding objectives.[10] In conflict and peace studies important distinctions are made between conflict management (containing a situation or limiting and reducing violent expressions of conflict), conflict resolution (resolving the underlying tensions and causes of conflict and so avoiding recurrence), and conflict transformation (changing the norms and views that instil conflict and the underlying structural issues, often through the pursuit of social justice). These are useful to consider when addressing different interventions or responses to conflict at all levels from the individual to the global. These approaches have been instrumental in informing many contemporary understandings of conflict in the social sciences and they have been an important part of the evolution of ideas, policies and programmes on the conflict and development agenda.[11] These disciplinary differences and skirmishes reflect not only the ways in which the nature of international security and conflict have taken shape in recent decades, but also the extent to which analysing international conflict is dynamic and contested work. It is this tension of ideas that is reflected in current debates about the role of aid in war-prone and war-torn countries and the extent to which development and peace can and should be separated from security and counter-insurgency strategies. One would also presume a natural fusion of theory and application, given the urgency of the subject matter. Yet academic–practitioner relations are at best wary and fuelled by mutual suspicion or, at worst, mutually dismissive. And among academics there are enduring differences about the role that theorists and researchers should play in engaging with policy makers and practitioners. Some believe the role of theorists is to interpret the world, not change it, while others support getting involved to the point of empowering particular groups and shaping policies (Nardin 1980; Jacoby 2008: 181–91).

Why development organisations became interested in war and peace

A greater relationship between conflict and development has emerged from the shifting political trends outlined earlier. This has rested on three main arguments. One argument for a relationship between international conflict and international development centres on violent conflict as a serious impediment to achieving the Millennium Development Goals (MDGs).[12] While there is not a specific goal related to conflict reduction or peace and security, subsequent reports and debates have highlighted the challenge for countries affected by conflict in reaching the MDGs (UN Millennium Project 2005). Thus protecting development gains is a motive for development agencies, NGOs and governments to be concerned about conflict in their strategies, funding and programmes (UNDP 2000; World Bank 2003).

A second and very influential argument for a relationship between conflict and development arises from the principle of 'do no harm' set out by Mary Anderson in her 1999 book of the same title. 'Do no harm' goes beyond the protecting development gains argument by highlighting the responsibility of development and aid actors not to cause, enable or exacerbate violent conflict through their policies and programmes. The idea of aid as merely technical, and development as essentially a positive process, is overturned and any pretence of neutrality in conflict-affected countries shattered. Recognised through this principle as a force for and driver of peace, development has first to be understood as interacting with conflict and knowing the precise possibilities of doing harm or good. This requires development policy makers, programme managers and NGOs to be more aware of conflict (Adams and Bradbury 1995). This shift in thinking was not without its detractors and resistance from professionals and activists used to working within long-term development time frames and pushing for sustainability of programming to end poverty – many of whom saw themselves as economists or technical specialists (in fields such as health, agriculture or education) and feared being drawn into front-line politics that would undermine development aims. It was also resisted by some in political and military roles who had hitherto viewed development as something that happened after war was long over, or as a resource to be deployed under political or military leadership in conflict situations.

A third argument for the relationship between conflict and development was that development was well-placed to address the underlying or *root causes* of violent conflict, often summarised as poverty, social injustice, and ethnic and group relations and tensions. While peacekeeping could hold the line between warring factions or accompany the early stages of implementation of a peace agreement, and while peace processes and diplomatic efforts could forge a peace agreement, development was seen as the answer to long-term conflict resolution because it addressed the structural issues of state, society and economy that underpinned violent conflict (Carnegie Commission 1997). As we will see in the next chapter, such presumptions of a causal relationship between development and conflict reduction are contested; and one rebuttal includes an argument that violent conflict can also bring political change and possibilities for alternative development (Agerbak 1992; Cramer 2006).

The development dimension of conflict prevention and peacebuilding has thus grown to include reorienting existing development programmes and building longer-term governance capacities in-country to resolve conflict and address its causes, triggers and long-term effects. Increasingly, development actors are learning the lessons of 'do no harm' by recognising the inherent need to 'mainstream' conflict sensitivity in their programmes, and to be innovative in their planning, if development resources are to be conscious resources of peacebuilding rather than hostages or fuel to conflict. The aim is to ensure development programmes in conflict-prone and post-conflict situations have the flexibility, responsiveness and context-specific analysis to lay the foundations for longer-term recovery, vulnerability reduction and prevention of recurrence of conflict. Such conflict-sensitive development requires aid actors to be more engaged with conflict dynamics and context instead of merely reacting to them. Directly addressing the causes of conflict is no longer simply about peace talks and mediation but also about addressing inequalities, weak governance, poverty and local insecurity that contribute to and result from violence and conflict. For development actors this has meant going beyond 'business as usual' and dealing with the political implications of aid in conflict-prone environments. For diplomats and political actors it has meant learning to 'do development' and understanding the importance and modalities of aid in supporting long-term peace and stability.

This evolution is usefully framed within the idea of 'working in, on or around' conflict. Working *around* conflict for development actors means 'business as usual' in terms of avoiding the conflict and withdrawing or suspending long-term programmes until the crisis is over, leaving the space to the humanitarian aid community to do the life-saving work. Working *in* conflict means development actors continuing to try to do something, even in conflict-prone areas. The focus is on integrating conflict-sensitivity into programmes on the premise of 'do no harm' so that social and economic policies and programmes can still be implemented but are re-oriented to take account of conflict risks. For example an ongoing agricultural programme might be modified to consider the balance of districts and groups with which it works, or to arrange gatherings in ways that take account of walking distances and routes where armed groups might be active. Working *on* conflict means addressing conflict prevention and peacebuilding directly through development programmes focused on particular causes and dynamics – for example, supporting demobilisation and reintegration programmes for ex-combatants; addressing reform of the security sector (police and armed forces); including civilian oversight through parliament as part of governance programming; or community-based livelihoods programmes aimed at bringing different groups together.[13] The principle of 'do no harm' provides the moral minimum, the floor beneath which international actors who intervene should not fall.

Yet an oft-repeated question reflecting an inherent dilemma for those seeking to do good is, 'Does aid fuel conflict and generate more harm than good?' This issue is termed the 'Nightingale risk', building on Florence Nightingale's objections to Henri

Dunant's establishment of the International Committee of the Red Cross in 1863 as an international humanitarian organisation based on the principles of impartiality and neutrality in providing life-saving assistance to soldiers and civilians on all sides of war. She (the pioneering nurse of field hospitals in the Crimean War) and he (the Swiss businessman affected by his experience of the Battle of Solferino) both personified the emerging humanitarian doctrine and its inherent dilemmas (Slim 2001; Hanlon 2006; Gourevitch 2010). In shaping the conflict and development agenda of the 1990s the Nightingale risk can be found in the cautionary tale of NGO and researcher voices (Uvin 1998; Anderson 1999) and also in the polemical attacks of journalists and politicians seeking an end to aid budgets.

The relationship between conflict and development is in the throes of critical reconsideration given the wider controversies that continue about aid effectiveness and calls to simply pull the plug. The pendulum swings violently between idealists and sceptics, from the relative high of the Make Poverty History campaign and the Gleneagles G8 Summit of 2005, where commitments to reach aid volumes of 0.7 per cent of GDP were wrung from donor governments, to the lows of allegations of widespread and systemic corruption and the drive for greater evidence and proof of impact that have fuelled a mounting media perception of wasted aid and impossible wars that are of little concern to Western/Northern societies. Some take issue with the effectiveness of aid and argue that it is not eradicating poverty and has become an industry (Easterly 2006; Riddell 2007; Glennie 2008), while others go further and question the basis of providing aid, particularly in countries and regions affected by widespread corruption or conflict (Wrong 2009; Polman 2010). That public funds for development assistance need to be accounted for and that those who spend the aid need to be accountable are beyond argument. However, as others have pointed out, accountability is not only financial. It extends to how aid is structured as a global industry and how development organisations and programmes have had a negative effect in prolonging conflict or providing cover to corruption and human rights abuses (de Waal 1997; Gourevitch 2010; Keen 2008; Le Billon 2003; Shearer 2000).

However, accountability is not only the preserve of donors, those who give the money, but also the world's poor, the displaced and the conflict-affected; the communities and people who are meant to benefit from aid in terms of reduced poverty, increased access to essential services, protection of human rights and longer-term sustainability of economic development and governance (implying functioning and accountable national administrations). Rarely is accountability understood or measured from below. Rarely do we ask those we claim to help how they experience international aid and what they think needs to be done to improve it. This can be said to be even more pronounced in conflict-affected countries where both the context and the nature of increasingly complex international interventions make it very difficult to establish shared objectives and participation of the affected communities in those interventions (Macrae 2001). Now more than ever (though there are strong historic and recent precedents) there is a resurgence of debates and arguments that aid should be directly tied to national interests in terms of business and security. Aid provided for its own sake, with a humanitarian ethos of 'care of distant strangers', can no longer be assumed to be a strong norm.

Another important trend for development actors is the way in which the post-9/11 agenda accelerated tensions within the global development community of academics, activists, bureaucrats and aid workers about the growing securitisation of aid. The new political agendas of terrorism and counterterrorism, failed and fragile states and the resurgence of statebuilding in third countries fuelled fears that development as an area of knowledge and practice dedicated to economic, social and even governance-related notions of sustainability and equity was being subsumed. The wars in Afghanistan and Iraq have compounded this as development and reconstruction work is very much on the front-line, and seen by some as part of the war and the peace.

2 | Greed, Grievance and Poverty: the Politics of Analysing Conflict

Politics or economics, genetics or environment, structure or agency – understanding war and violence has been a battle of ideas about how to bring about order, society, peace and equality since antiquity, from Thucydides' account of the Peloponnesian War through to the two twentieth-century World Wars that gave rise to the current international system of peace and security set out in the UN Charter of 1945. It may seem self-evident that how a conflict situation is defined or mapped out has an important bearing on the responses to it, but the explanation of violent conflict remains a contested field of theory and practice. This chapter discusses ideas about the causes and drivers of contemporary violent conflict and the theories of change that lie behind them. It focuses on the academic and policy ideas that have shaped conflict analysis as a practice: from biological determinism and psychological theories of individual and group dynamics to notions of structural violence, horizontal inequalities, 'greed and grievance', and linkages between poverty and conflict.

A range of persistent explanations and theories of conflict convey how these debates have taken shape in the second half of the last century and into the early decades of this one.

Explaining conflict: three key debates

One set of debates concerns whether conflict is *inherent* or *contingent*. If it is inherent in humans, then the challenge is to mitigate, contain, manage or reduce such tendencies. If it *is contingent*, and therefore arising from particular settings and social processes (some of them sudden and aberrant), then other questions arise. Can conflict be unlearned, or shaped to more positive and peaceful alternatives (Webb 1986)? Inherency can be explained in terms of the 'way things are': the assumption is that for biological, evolutionary psychological, or culturally determined reasons aggression and violence are inherent in the human condition and part of the nature of human beings and society. In terms of theories discussed below, both socio-biology and cultural determinism reflect this perspective. More contingent theories include the frustration/aggression hypothesis and relative deprivation. These focus on the circumstances rather than human nature and are based on the rationale that conflict can be overcome through a better understanding of processes.

A second set of debates on the explanation of violent conflict concerns *objectivist* versus *subjectivist* perspectives. This debate reflects a fundamental division in social science knowledge claims: does *structure* or *agency* have the greater role in determining social action and understanding? The *objectivist* position refers to the potentially structural nature of violent conflict and the need to look at institutions, systems and dynamics that lie behind overt and latent (discussed in more detail below) or hidden conflict. From this perspective conflict may be observed even if participants are not aware of it or expressing it. Examples of such conflict include slavery, sexism and caste systems. The *subjectivist* position holds that conflict exists when any or all of the parties/agents involved express an incompatibility of goals. The conflict is deemed to be resolved when there is no longer a perception of incompatibility. For

Continued

example, a strike by workers for better pay because of felt grievance of low wages is resolved when a pay increase is granted and the workers no longer feel there is a source of conflict.

A third set of debates arises from *political economy* explanations of violent conflict, captured in the 'greed versus grievance' debate that has been very influential in shaping development discourses on conflict. The focus on war economies as both cause and result of conflict raises the issue of the role that poverty plays in the cause and the course of wars and violent conflict. One would expect this to be the dominant explanation of a relationship between conflict and development, and yet the evidence remains contested, and the linkages are often expressed as indirect. So, if conflict is not caused by poverty, what is the role of development in responding to conflict situations?

Sociobiology

In the battle over scarce resources, aggression – 'a tendency to engage in hostile and intentionally destructive acts' (Davies 1980: 29) – is one behaviour that has evolved to ensure survival. This explanation of conflict as innate and inherent draws ultimately on Charles Darwin's theorisation of evolution. More recently the biologist E. O. Wilson sought to learn and apply lessons from the animal world to human evolution and behaviour. He asserted that '[a]ggression is genetic in the sense ... that its components have proved to have a high degree of heritability and are therefore subject to evolution' (1975: 248–9). In humans it may well be 'adaptive – that is, programmed to increase the survival and reproductive performance of individuals thrown into stressful situations' (ibid.: 255). It is this instinctual and evolutionary perspective that also influenced the work of ethnologist Konrad Lorenz (1966), focusing on the behavioural study of aggression in animals where conflict is seen as part of the process of natural selection – the survival of the fittest – in strengthening the gene pool and the ability of individuals and groups to survive. Aggression cannot be avoided but can only be channelled in more constructive ways – and indeed, by this argument, to some extent one cannot be responsible for aggression, given its spontaneous and innate nature. This is a very instrumental interpretation of human behaviour that extrapolates from animals to humans with no consideration of complex mobilising social actions and inter-actions, nor of the roles of identity formation, assumptions of gender, and other categories in defining actions and behaviours. In addition to this criticism, the underlying science was also much-criticised for its political and ideological positions in terms of serving the cause of genetic manipulation and social control through such programmes as eugenics, population control, racial and gender categorisation of inferiority, and other justifications for discrimination (Webb 1992; Allen et al. 1978). And yet the Hobbesian notion that conflict and strife are part of human nature – where life is nasty, brutish and short, and where, in the absence of strong rule, humanity will descend into a state of war – is a belief that endures and still influences international debates on the nature of war and how best to prevent conflict and build peace.

Structural violence

Structural violence is a core concept of conflict analysis and is associated with the work of Norwegian peace researcher Johan Galtung (1969), one of the founders of the field of peace studies. Structural violence, he argued, is not direct or personal like physical or psychological violence; it is more often implicit, normalised and often institutionalised through forms of exploitation, inequality, oppression or discrimination that are implicit (and sometimes intentional) forms of violence against particular groups or individuals. Poverty, disease and sexism all become forms of violence in this context. To deny people their human needs – looking beyond life and food to include dignity, justice and equality – is a source of violence. When people are prevented from reaching their potential and are denied opportunities to fulfil basic needs that reasonably should be met, this is a form of violence and conflict. This understanding of violence defines the *objectivist* view of conflict, and exerted great influence on more activist-driven forms of peace research. It may also explain why conflicts can sometimes remain latent. Proponents of an extreme version of this view argue in support of certain acts of violence or conflict that serve to make structural forms of violence more explicit. This may be linked to Marxist ideas of 'false consciousness', where the oppressed are assumed to be unaware of their oppression and the violence of systems that entrap them. However, not all structuralists are Marxists – as in the case of the first Chair of Peace Studies in Britain, Quaker writer and mediator Adam Curle. The pursuit of equality and social justice is at the heart of a peace agenda, and the notion of structural violence informs the central distinction between *negative* and *positive* peace (Galtung 1969; Curle 1971) – the need to understand peace as more than a situation of non-war. Negative peace refers to the cessation of hostilities and the ending of overt violence. A ceasefire is a clear example of such an outcome. Positive peace seeks to go beyond the absence of violence; it implies that underlying causes and dynamics of violent conflict have been addressed to prevent a recurrence of violence and to build a peaceful future. In the tradition of structuralists, this means addressing the social, economic and political forms of structural violence that shape inequalities and injustices as bases of conflict.

Cultural inherency

Cultural and historical determinism define nationality and ethnicity as the shaping of a will to power and violence in pursuit of fixed and primary identities. This is the broad and widely circulated notion that underpins assumptions of the inherency of conflict among particular groups. Nationalism in concept and practice is the ready repository of such debates, where the notions of nation, ethnicity, tradition and identity are the subject of controversy and debate in terms of the origins, construction and modernity of nationalism and claims of identity linked to territory.[1] The resurgence of nationalist conflicts with the end of the Cold War and the opening up of the former Soviet Union and Eastern Europe led to the re-emergence of notions of primordial and essential identities; a common perception was that the Cold War superstructure had kept the lid on ethnic conflicts that now suddenly re-erupted. 'Ethnic cleansing' in Bosnia re-ignited the view of nations and ethnicity as somehow essential and inherent; ethnic conflict became shorthand for internecine, internal wars in very unstable countries, ranging from Somalia, Bosnia-Herzegovina and Liberia to the full horror of genocide in Rwanda. In the 1990s these conflicts became the touchstone not only for humanitarian intervention but also for an analysis of their causes and dynamics as barbaric, tribal and historic grievances that had been unleashed by the end of the Cold War (Kaplan 1993; 1994; Keegan 1993). This analysis of 'barbarism' was played out in endless media coverage explaining the new wars through economic explanations of neo-liberal globalisation; predatory, utilitarian or greed discourses; and post-Cold War insecurity. In response, more hawkish proponents of liberal interventionism espoused resurgent ideas of trusteeship[2] – taking ungovernable countries back under international control in ways that had been considered obsolete following the wave of decolonisation between the 1950s and the

1980s – and the need for strong international control of countries considered unfit to manage their own affairs (Cooper 2003). However, as others have argued, this over-simplified notion of inherent and irrational tendencies to conflict does not explain why conflicts break out in some places and not in others, why some situations are more violent and intractable than others, and how factors other than ethnic identity enable insurgency to take root (Brown 2001; Fearon and Laitin 2003).

The relationship between ethnic identities and nationalism, considered thus far in terms of essential inherency, can also be explained through a constructivist approach. While Anthony Smith (1991; 1993) does not subscribe to a biologically driven primordial interpretation of ethnic groups, nations and national-ism, he does assert an understanding of ethnic identities as cultur-ally inherent in terms of creating and forming communities based on membership, kinship and shared customs and traditions from generation to generation. Ethnicity is not necessarily 'natural' or a given, but does have long historical roots in the development of myth and memories, including wars and conflicts, that forge the *ethnie* (ethnic community) into an ethnic identity that continues over time. More constructivist writers such as Benedict Anderson (1991 [1983]) take the view that identities (including national ones) are made, remade and produced through various processes to create 'imagined communities' to which people attach and identify. Identity thus, to greater and lesser extent, is a social pro-cess of constant creation, re-creation and reproduction. Meaning is given in interaction with others and with the world. The context is as important as the origin for self-identification, and this process is not rigid or presumed but dynamic and shifting.

In terms of global conflict Samuel P. Huntington's hyperbolic 'clash of civilisations' hypothesis reflects an essentialist vision of territorially defined areas where modernity confronts tradition, and this difference becomes the basis for a conflict-prone world order (1993; 1996). He argues that in the post-Cold War era international conflict has moved beyond the contestation of kingdoms, states and ideologies (the past 300 years) and that we now live in an age when 'civilisation identity' is the most salient factor for potential conflict. Huntington identifies eight civilisations of the new global era that include Western, Confucian, Islamic, Hindu, Slavic-Orthodox, Latin American and *possibly* (he says) an African civilisation. Religion is singled out for particular reference by Huntington as a form of civilisation identity; he adduces an historical determinism and inevitability about conflict between the West and Islam in particular. While he criticises Western policies and positioning in the world, Huntington also singles out Islamic civilisation for promoting conflict, as in his infamous statement that 'Islam has bloody borders' (1993: 35). This 'clash of civilisations' thinking was very influential on the neo-conservative architects of the US response to the terrorist attacks in New York in 2001; it helped to shape a view of Islam as particularly warlike, fundamentalist and aggressive. Counter-arguments and debates have ensued to modify this reductionism and put militant variants of Islamic politics in context, reminding us that mobilisation remains critical to understanding violent conflict, and that while explanations such as a cultural inherency in nations may seek to describe groups as given, they do not fully explain how we move from groups to conflict (Jacoby 2008: 79–81).

Grievance and relative deprivation

The *frustration/aggression* hypothesis draws on the work of Freud and others to suggest that aggression is the consequence of frustration, and that frustration always leads to aggression even if that aggression is then displaced or sublimated by the individual. While aggression is not innate, the potential for aggression is an 'innate capacity' (Dollard et al. (1988 [1939]). It is classified as a contingent theory as it relates to the behaviour of individuals in response to external influences. The hypothesis proposes that a sense of grievance results from unmet expectations and from impediments to the fulfilment of needs and goals. So, for example, hunger or poverty can lead individuals to be prepared to attack the sources they might believe to be preventing their access to food, cash or income. However, there may also be displacement of this aggression (domestic abuse is sometimes interpreted in this way, as is scapegoating of 'others' as discussed later in group dynamics) if the cost of following through is too high (for example, arrest and imprisonment or personal harm). Levels of personal control and choice are assumed in reducing frustration and the likelihood of violence. Criticism has centred on the overly broad interpretation of aggression and its linear logic, as there are a number of responses possible to frustration of which overt aggression is only one – avoidance, apathy or constructive coping are examples (Miller 1965; Zimmerman 1983). Furthermore, frustration requires some cues or intervening variables before aggression becomes the chosen action. These can include a move through anger toward aggression and the presence of weapons that make violence more likely. Aggression also results not just from frustration but from other sources, including reaction to an attack or to pain. It can be instrumental (using violence as a means to an end), taught (as in the controlled aggression of military training for combat) and also socially circumscribed (as when an individual is 'caught up' in violence even though not frustrated personally, as in riots,). The hypothesis is based on individual behaviour and does not take account of contexts of social conflict or consider how individuals might organise for violence. However, it provides the basis on which others have developed more nuanced ideas of human needs, expectations and the formation of grievances as aspects of conflict analysis – the 'why' of conflict. It also provides a template for learning about behavioural change towards non-violence and conflict prevention.

Building on frustration/aggression, Ted Gurr (1970) applied the theory of *relative deprivation*, outlined in his classic text *Why Men Rebel*, to develop a social psychological model of mobilisation for political violence. He contended that conflict was a function of rising expectations not being met and that this leads to a 'want–get' gap (the gap between expectations and capabilities) that can trigger conflict; it provides a perspective on the agency of actors and what prompts them to rise up. Growing expectations involve a sense of comparison where individuals and groups see themselves as less well off than others around them, as in times of rapid economic growth or even recession, when groups may feel others are coping better or not suffering as much. A lack of opportunity and unequal distribution of benefits of growth or costs of recession can trigger unrest. Even when growth is buoyant, if the capabilities (of government and the economy) to satisfy expectations do not keep pace, then frustration and the possibility of unrest will emerge. Criticisms of Gurr's theory relate to how far solidarity can be assumed to result from relative deprivation, and when the gap between expectations and capabilities can be considered sufficient to trigger a conflict response (Scott 1977: 236). This social-scientific application of ideas of sociology, psychology and politics was influential, however, in the context of historical and structural explanations in a new field of enquiry called 'peasant studies' which focused on the nature, causes and processes of revolution-ary movements.[3] Both frustration/aggression and relative depriva-tion approaches offer some insight into the 'why' of conflict by way of the emergence of 'grievance' as a reason to engage in violence.

In further consideration of *group dynamics* we can move beyond the level of the individual in terms of presumed biological, cultural and psychological predisposition to aggression and conflict, and seek to understand how more collective or group-based forms of conflict and violence develop and emerge. This suggests that conflict may not be inherent but may have more to do with environment and learning. These are often discussed in terms of cognitive psychological processes that help to support the positive and coherent self-image of a group (the in-group), partly through negative attitudes and perceptions of rival groups (the out-groups) (Mitchell 1981: 97; Coser 1956). It can be argued that some conflict has the positive function of creating group cohesion. The self-image processes include selective perception and recall of events or history to favour one's own group, and positive identification of self with the group; the out-group processes include stereotyping, scapegoating and, in the extreme case, dehumanisation that enables all manner of violence. Examples include the stigmatisation and vilification of Jewish communities by the Nazi regime in Germany before and during the Second World War; the anti-immigrant basis of many new extreme-right parties in Europe, including the Flemish Vlaams Belang in Belgium and the British National Party in the UK; and the mainstream rhetoric supporting recent expulsions of groups of Roma people from Italy and France. In fact, propaganda in any conflict relies on nurturing one's own virile self-image and denigrating the 'other' as less than, as different, as dangerous.[4] Even a casual glance at coverage of the conflicts in Northern Ireland, Sri Lanka and Bosnia-Herzegovina shows how potent group dynamics and identification can be. At the global level one also witnesses such dynamics in the mirror-imaging of the superpowers (US and USSR) during the Cold War, when mutually negative views often matched exactly (Mitchell 1981: 111–14). In the so-called 'War on Terror' in the aftermath of 9/11, and the rise of the new conservatives during the administration of President George W. Bush, a similar mirroring prevailed in the depiction by US (and some broader Western) constituencies of Islamic militant groups and their followers.

Such imagery is difficult to target or contain, as it spills over to whole group representations; in the end, there is a general failure to distinguish between moderate and extreme Islamic views or politics or, in the reciprocating vision, between extreme white Christian conservatism and the wider spectrum of US views, types and political positions. *Conflict attitudes* therefore develop and can be nurtured and mobilised for more overt and violent conflict. This explanation falls within the subjectivist category: analysts seek to expand on how actors are shaped for conflict behaviour; invoke the assumption that environment plays a role; and argue that change is possible through actions such as increased communication to reduce misperceptions of groups, self-reflection and questioning, mediation to open up understanding, or confidence-building measures designed to enable people to meet across divides. The role of education and communication is seen as important here.

Greed and economic essentialism

The role of economics in interpreting conflict and analysing its causes has enjoyed a resurgence and exerted considerable policy influence on development approaches to conflict through the work of Paul Collier (2001; 2008), the Oxford professor who has also led research at the World Bank. His original paper with Anke Hoeffler (2000) on 'Greed and Grievance in Civil Wars' provides a model of contemporary civil wars (wars within states that cause at least 1,000 battle-related deaths) in particular, and claims to demonstrate that greed trumps grievance as a motivation of war, and that international responses need to be reconsidered in that light. Based on an analysis of 44 wars across 34 countries (from an original dataset of 161 countries), Collier and Hoeffler elaborate a model of explanation for the causes of these civil wars that centres on the predatory actions of armed groups for gain and profit. They suggest three major characteristics of countries undergoing civil wars from their research: an economy that is at least 25 per cent reliant on primary commodity exports (diamonds, rubber, coltan and other natural assets); low average income in the country; and slow economic growth. Other characteristics that increase the likelihood of violent conflict are:

- dispersal of population across wide areas (for example, eastern parts of DRC);
- if the country has recently emerged from war (it is here that the widely cited figure arises of some 40 per cent of countries relapsing into conflict within five years of a ceasefire or peace agreement);
- low school enrolment rates for male youth population and a high proportion of male youth within the entire population;
- a large diaspora in the US that can fund and fuel the conflict – this is a risk factor particularly in the early period of post-conflict.

These factors, they argue, lead to rebel organisations being established more in line with organised crime structures on a large scale rather than protest movements. Rebel groups are engaged in looting and extortion (at different points in the extraction and transport processes for natural resources) to fund and fuel conflict. The predatory drive to loot and profit makes war a lucrative business; once afoot, there are few incentives or punitive threats to abandon it. The protracted war in Angola is the classic case, with the UNITA-controlled diamond fields at its heart; and it is matched today by the market for coltan mined in the east of Congo, along with diamonds, gold and cassiterite.

Collier and Hoeffler categorically dismiss the explanatory value of the grievance model, which is defined by proxy factors of income inequality (and so, relative poverty); lack of democratic rights; and religious and ethnic difference and diversity. In fact, they contend that such diversity contributes to reduced conflict.[5] They argue that grievances are a by-product of conflict, manufactured by armed groups to maintain the popular bases of support and labour needed to ensure the continued looting – and as such do not have an objective basis. They conclude that addressing grievances will not necessarily end the conflict. Indeed the manufactured grievances drive the conflict further and create wider appeal for conflict, so leaving such countries in what Collier in *The Bottom Billion* (2008) presents as a 'conflict trap' that keeps the world's poorest populations in poverty. Greed versus grievance is thus a utilitarian approach that reframes conflict analysis and poses a different question: rather than asking 'why people rebel', the question is, 'What are the gains and who gains in rebellions and civil wars?' The model has been criticised – and its assailants include other political and development economists – as being overly reductionist of factors that cause and drive conflicts; using weak proxies in representing social factors such as mobilisation, grievance and participation in civil wars; and failing to capture the dynamics of change in violent conflict as a structural and relational reality (Cramer 2002; Keen 2008: 25–49). Nonetheless, the greed thesis has been very influential in shaping donor thinking on conflict, and is aligned with the growth of a security and development agenda in prioritising responses that address the threat of armed groups. Both the 'new wars' debates and the greed thesis, while emerging from very different analytical standpoints, have influenced a very reductionist view of conflict and intervention. They offer a

Conflict Diamonds

The UN defines conflict diamonds as 'diamonds that originate from areas controlled by forces or factions opposed to legitimate and internationally recognised governments, and are used to fund military action in opposition to those governments, or in contravention of the decisions of the Security Council'. Trends that define this trade include armed groups extorting 'taxes' from companies at various points in the production and supply chain of diamonds – or in some cases taking over operations themselves – to make arms purchases and fund and fuel conflict in various ways. International companies or their local partners enter the picture, too: profiting from the chaos of war to gain mining conccessions and favourable terms when market information and regulation has broken down; smuggling primary products through third countries to access international markets and disguise provenance; and hiring known corrupt businesspeople and politicians to act as brokers. Conflict diamonds are also referred to as 'blood diamonds'. The issue received global attention and publicity in the 2006 film *Blood Diamond*, centred on Sierra Leone.

Kimberley Process

The UN General Assembly adopted Resolution A/Res/55/56 on conflict diamonds in 2001 and supported an international rough diamond certification regime that became known as the Kimberley Process for Certification. It was formally launched in 2003 to verify and certify the origin of diamonds and marked a success story for campaigners who had worked to raise awareness regarding the mining and trade of diamonds from war zones in Angola, Sierra Leone and the Democratic Republic of Congo. Notable campaign landmarks were the 1998 report by Global Witness, a campaigning NGO on natural resources and conflict, titled *A Rough Trade: The Role of Governments and Companies in the Angolan Conflict* and the 2000 report by Partnership Africa Canada (PAC), a non-profit organisation that supports research and policy dialogue in Africa, titled *The Heart of the Matter: Sierra Leone, Diamonds and Human Security.*

The actors involved in the Kimberley Process include civil society organisations such as Global Witness and Partnership Africa Canada, the United Nations and the World Diamond Council (an industry organisation created in response to increased political pressure and adverse publicity regarding conflict diamonds). See http://www.diamondfacts.org/index-2.html. Seventy-five governments have adopted the certification process. However the Kimberley Process remains dogged by accusations of weak monitoring and results as reports continue of third countries (for example Ghana in the case of Côte d'Ivoire) being used to channel conflict diamonds to the legal trade. Industry claims estimate that the trade in conflict diamonds was never more than 4 per cent of global trade and has been reduced to less than 1 per cent.

Another business-focused response is the OECD Guidelines for Multinational Enterprises, last revised in 2000. It is a voluntary code of business ethics to promote responsible business conduct by ensuring compliance with international standards, including human rights and environmental impact. These Guidelines are currently being updated to reflect due diligence on awareness and risks related to supply chains of products and services. Forty-two governments are signed up to the Guidelines: see http://www.oecd.org/about/0,3347,en_2649_34889_1_1_1_1_ 1,00.html

In 2005 the UN appointed Professor John Ruggie as Special Representative of the Secretary-General on human rights and trans-national corporations and other business enterprises. Under his auspices the Protect, Respect and Remedy: a Framework for Business and Human Rights was developed and adopted by the United Nations Human Rights Council in 2008. This focuses on the roles and responsibilities of states, businesses and civil society to build a viable framework that includes the corporate responsibility to protect and respect human rights through, inter alia, due diligence in management practices of human resources, security, and supply chains.

Sources: Global Witness (1998); UN (2003, 2008, 2009b); OECD (2000); PAC (2000); Le Billon (2001)

utilitarian view of conflict and violence based on resource extraction, criminality, and supply chains – and yet may also be said to reinforce the 'new barbarism' they seek to challenge with their combination of hyper-economic rationality driving often vicious violence. Policy responses for Collier and Hoeffler include greater transparency of markets for primary commodity exports to prevent the sale of looted produce; sanctions against groups and individuals known to benefit from conflict trade; and cutting off support to rebel groups from outside the country. (Keen (2008: 29) also notes, tongue in cheek, one implication of their utilitarian analysis: given the variable of mountainous terrain as a factor of conflict, he suggests, levelling mountains might be a policy recommendation to consider.)

Yet the 'dismal science' of economics has a longer history of explaining revolt and rebellion, not least within the field of peasant studies in the 1960s and 1970s – when debate also raged around the structural (objectivist) versus agency (subjectivist) theories of explanation. The political anthropologist James Scott, in reviewing these debates, suggests that '[a]ny theory of revolution must make a place for the anger, revenge, hatred that are so obviously a part of the experience. Marketplace bargaining metaphors miss this entirely. If such emotions are not to be considered acts of pure madness, we are forcibly brought to the living moral economy of the participants' (1977: 240). Political economist Chris Cramer echoes this when he argues that 'rational choice theories of conflict typically lay waste to specificity and contingency … they sack the social and … even in their individualism they violate the complexity of individual motivation, razing the individual (and key groups) down to monolithic maximising agents' (2002: 1846). There is a wider field of research beyond the greed thesis that focuses on the political economy of war and addresses the structure and dynamics of war economies that are part of protracted violent conflict. Writers highlight themes including the role of the global arms trade, the role of political predatory elites, weak states with poor services, and a community-based focus on livelihoods and survival strategies (Cramer 2002; 2006; Berdal and Malone 2000; Duffield 2001; Keen 2005; Stewart, Fitzgerald et al. 2001). This wider view includes the self-critical aspect of the political economy of war in terms of the role of humanitarian and development assistance itself in potentially creating market distortions and incentives for corruption and gain, as well as sustenance of fighters that may fuel and drive violent conflict even as it brings assistance and relief to civilians and victims of war. A *cause célèbre* within the political economy focus has been 'conflict diamonds' (see box above).

The war economies literature reveals the limits of current mapping of conflicts and brings into view new actors (arms dealers, border guards, armed groups), organisations (global corporations, local businesses and money exchanges, criminal networks and drug cartels), and levels of operation (cross-border, sub-regional, global, South–South, South–North) that test the limits of international policy making and responses to peace, security and development. However, this does not prove that greed is the only motive or dynamic of war that matters. Not everyone profits from war, and survival is more often the dream, not profit, for people whose lives are torn apart by war. Rather than a trade-off of greed and grievance we need to engage complexity in drawing on the range of theories and arguments in particular contexts.

The relationship between poverty and violent conflict

The relationship between poverty and conflict would seem to be a natural area of enquiry into why international development resources and policies should be concerned with violent conflict. The case for poverty as a cause and consequence of violent conflict has been contentious. Academics and policy makers share a reluctance to state a causal relationship. This is underpinned by a consensus that causality between income inequality and conflict is difficult to establish on empirical grounds, given weak and difficult-to-access data in war-prone environments and the limited nature of standard measures such as the Gini co-efficient. Being poor is not automatically a cause of violent conflict (Cramer 2003; Collier 2001; 2008). An analysis of league tables produced to rank conflict-affected and poor countries raises some interesting points of comparison and contradiction: the poorest countries are not always necessarily in conflict, while some middle-income countries can be in varying states of war and post-war recovery.

When more multi-dimensional understandings and measures of poverty, beyond income and econometrics, are considered, it can be argued that the interrelationship of poverty and violent conflict can be reviewed in greater depth. For example, relative deprivation as an explanation of mobilisation would signal that poverty and conflict are somehow in relationship in terms of how poor one is relative to one's neighbours. An interesting and influential variation in relative deprivation analysis has been provided by Frances Stewart's work on 'horizontal inequalities', where group-based regional, ethnic or communal position and identity – rather than differences between individuals (which is classified as a vertical inequality) – are argued to have greater salience in defining relative deprivation as a feature of conflict for the individual (2003; 2008). Commonly used measurements of poverty (notably the Gini coefficient) measure vertical inequality in terms of comparing individuals and households, and focus on income inequality in defining relative poverty. According to Stewart, however, they do not take account of group affiliations and welfare as shaping the experience of the individual in ways that go beyond income and include access to a range of social, economic and political goods. Examples of horizontal inequalities that have led to violent expressions of conflict include Sri Lanka (between the Tamil minority and Sinhalese majority); Northern Ireland (between the Protestant majority and Catholic minority); and Burundi and Rwanda (between the Hutu majority and the Tutsi minority). The role for horizontal inequalities, however, relies on a strong correlation between communal identity and grievance based on persistent discrimination – and so, while it can explain some conflict, it needs to be considered as another factor for analysing or predicting conflict but not necessarily on its own. A multi-dimensional approach to the relationship of poverty and conflict also underpins the argument that violent conflict is likely to be a 'driver' or 'maintainer' of chronic poverty, passing from one generation to the next with implications for a cycle of poverty and conflict that is difficult to break. This approach is supported by efforts to highlight the indirect costs of conflict such as the collapse of the state, lack of access to medical and other essential services, the shift to an informal economy and subsistence strategies, the collapse of livelihoods and the rise in female-headed households (Goodhand 2001; 2003).

Politically speaking, debates on modernity and conflict have long considered that development itself can 'do harm' and bring forth inequalities or structural changes that enable rather than reduce conflict. Huntington, before he became (in)famous for his 'clash of civilisations', wrote a very influential work on *The Political Order of Changing Societies* (1968) where he argues precisely this. In some sense this is the self-evident claim that conflict is always present alongside change and growth, and that it is the management of conflict constructively and the prevention of violent conflict that become the issue. Cramer takes an interesting view of the rationality of civil wars in his critique of liberal notions of peace and economic development by focusing on

How do global league tables rank peace, poverty and conflict?

The Global Peace Index (GPI) was launched in 2007 by an Australia-based global think tank, the Institute for Economics and Peace, which focuses on the interrelationship of economic development, business and peace. The GPI seeks to measure economic, cultural and institutional drivers for peace to promote the 'absence of violence' as positive and negative peace (as understood by Galtung and discussed on p. 24). The Economist Intelligence Unit collaborates in collating the data for 23 indicators across 149 countries that have been developed with the critical inputs of an international advisory panel drawn from various peace research and think tank backgrounds. These indicators range across three baskets of issues: conflict-related (incidents of conflict, etc.); society-related (perceptions of insecurity, crime, etc.); and militarisation (arms spending, cost of UN peacekeeping, etc.). The GPI for 2010 ranks New Zealand as the most peaceful country, followed by Iceland, Japan, Austria and Norway in the top five. Some 15 of the top 20 countries are in Western or Central Europe. Iraq is the least peaceful country, at the bottom of the table, just behind Somalia (148), Afghanistan, Sudan, Pakistan, Israel, Russia, Georgia, Chad, and the Democratic Republic of Congo (140).

The Failed States Index (FSI) has been produced since 2004 by a US-based research and policy organisation – the Fund for Peace – with the magazine *Foreign Policy*. The Index ranks 177 countries across 12 social, economic, political, and military indicators that include demographic pressures, flows of refugees and internally displaced persons (IDPs), sharp economic decline, uneven development aligned to groups, security apparatus, factionalised elites, and human rights. Somalia tops the 2009 index, followed by a top 10 that includes Zimbabwe, Sudan, Chad, Democratic Republic of Congo, Iraq, Afghanistan, Central Africa Republic, Guinea, and Pakistan; six of the top ten countries are in sub-Saharan Africa. The FP analysis cites exclusively internal reasons for state failure and does not look to the regional or global context for external factors or interventions that weaken states or generate instability. It concedes that 'geopolitical considerations' may well determine that more attention is paid to Pakistan than to Guinea.

The UN Human Development Report is a reference guide for development policy makers and practitioners that celebrated its twentieth year in 2010. The HDR features the Human Development Index (HDI), which is effectively a league table of the world's states according to levels of poverty based on national income, but also extending to indicators – such as infant and maternal mortality, and primary education enrolment – that relate to living standards, health and education. In 2009, it listed the HDI for 182 out of the 192 UN member states. The bottom ten countries, listed in descending order, were Guinea-Bissau, Burundi, Chad, Democratic Republic of Congo, Burkina Faso, Mali, Central Africa Republic, Sierra Leone, Afghanistan and Niger. Seven of these countries are experiencing or have recently experienced violent conflict and nine of the countries are in sub-Saharan Africa. So we can say that there seems to be a correlation between poverty and conflict.

However, there are anomalies about the HDI methodology in terms of reflecting the interaction of insecurity and poverty. For example, the Occupied Territories sits in the medium HDI level at 110, even though it is a very insecure and unsafe environment for many of its inhabitants and a source of great immediate and regional insecurity and violent conflict. Again, Sudan, Nepal, Indonesia, Sri Lanka, Pakistan, Fiji and Myanmar are all middle-ranked in the HDI, though all display particular risks and experience of insecurity and violent conflict. Lebanon and Colombia feature in the 'high human development' section and yet are beset with internal and regional insecurities, conflicts and violence. On the other hand, not all the low-ranking HDI countries are synonymous with violent conflict or risk of conflict. This serves to underline the fact that while poverty and conflict can interact in some instances with very devastating consequences (Iraq and Somalia are not ranked and listed under 'other UN member states'), poverty is not an exclusive measure of conflict and insecurity. Other factors need to be taken into account and tracked alongside measures of poverty.

The countries common to the top 10 of the FSI and the bottom 10 of the HDI and the GPI are Afghanistan, Chad, and Democratic Republic of Congo.

Sources: SIPRI (2009, 2010); UN (2009a); Failed States Index (2009); GPI (2010)

violent conflict as not simply a negative or diseased abnormality, but as a generator of change and transformation in what he terms the 'paradox of violence and war' where 'violence destroys but is also often associated with social creativity' (2006: 279). Therefore, beyond economics, understanding poverty and conflict needs to be seen as a complex interplay of social, economic, political, geographic, historical and environmental factors that generate possibilities and scenarios for violent conflict in certain situations.

All of the theories outlined here give us indications about factors of conflict (political, economic, historical, and psychological) and levels of conflict (personal, group, state, regional and global). In reality most situations of violent conflict may reflect any or all of these factors. We can see instances where modern responses to war and development would find resonance with different and sometimes contradictory explanations outlined here. For example, in revolutionary and anti-colonial wars both structural violence and relative deprivation reasoning might fit. These explanations could also apply to the scenario that development itself and the early modernisation theories that drove it (and still resonate) created conflicts when the rising tide did not lift all boats – leading to political struggles for access to power, land, and a push for greater social and economic reform and change. The 'new wars' are interpreted on one hand (reflecting cultural determinism) as essentially ethnic and inevitable wars with inherent primitivism shaping perceptions and responses, and on the other (in terms of structural violence and an objectivist definition of conflict) as a direct result and reaction to globalisation and the impact of neo-liberal economic policies of structural adjustment, unfair trade and international development assistance flows that have weakened emerging state structures in the Global South, where poor regional integration and influence by non-state actors (military and economic) are driving conflict for natural resources and control of weak states.

In evaluating the relevance and usefulness of conflict theories in shaping political and development responses to war there is a need to overcome the somewhat false polarisation of structure and agency (objectivist and subjectivist) to get us beyond the tyranny of empiricism and the presumed exclusivity of particular explanations of theories. For example, international relations theorist Vivienne Jabri (1996) applies Antony Giddens's structuration theory to such ends, and highlights the continuities rather than the exceptionalism of war and violence. Anthropological approaches and theories have also re-emerged to open up the viability of research and studies to build a better understanding, grounded in extensive fieldwork, of modern armed conflict and the continuities of violence (Nordstrom 1997; Richards 1996; 2005). For example, Carolyn Nordstrom (2004; 2007) through her innovative use of ethnography, opens up these human aspects – the agency that underlies the structures of war economies and goes beyond known boundaries of states, organisations and societies. From the youth-soldier in Mozambique to the arms dealers who provide the guns, and the diamond smugglers who fund the trade for guns, she unearths the complexity of contemporary war and violence that is about both structures and people. The sociologist Siniša Malešević (2010: 2) offers 'a sociology of war and violence' that he claims has been absent from debates and explanations of contemporary large-scale violent conflict. He privileges the role of the organisation of coercion and generation of mass-based ideology as vital social processes that underpin collective violence and are premised on the contention that 'it is our sociality, not individuality which makes us both compassionate altruists and enthusiastic killers'.

3 | Using Conflict Analysis Frameworks

> It is quite possible that a project may fail according to limited developmental criteria but succeed according to broader peacebuilding criteria .... It is [also] possible that a project may succeed according to pre-determined developmental criteria but fail in terms of a beneficial impact on peace. (Bush 1998: 6)

The mapping of conflict remains both challenging and necessary if understanding and responses are to be developed. The range of theories presented in Chapter 2 highlights the complexity not only of conflict situations themselves but also of the potential number of responses and interventions that can be advocated. There are many coexisting explanations of what causes and drives violent conflict: enough to remind any analyst that mapping out conflict situations and scenarios is always a daunting challenge – but one that has to be met if responses are to be relevant, inclusive and effective. The task is one of tracking dynamism and not allowing the conflict to be taken as a single snapshot at a given moment, but rather to be sequenced as a film that moves: conflict analysis should edit and capture the back story, the key events, the actors and their complex interactions over time. The politics of analysis and interpretation remains a live issue in terms of the theories of change that underlie different responses; otherwise, as Jacoby (2008: 81) concludes, 'if violence and conflict are eternal and immutable, the best that can be hoped for in policy terms is … a programme of defensive securitisation'.

Yet a view of conflict as amenable to an understanding of various causes, triggers and actors *can* give rise to policy options for the mitigation and prevention of conflict, and also the lasting transformation of the causes of conflict to actively promote peace as a feasible outcome. Policy prescriptions differ in shaping interventions and responses. This need to better understand and better respond to situations of increasingly internecine, dispersed and chronic violent conflicts drove the search, in the 1990s and 2000s, for development interventions that could support other conflict prevention, peacemaking and peacebuilding processes, and at the very least avoid becoming part of the conflict itself. Conflict analysis and assessment tools became part of development planning in this drive for conflict-sensitive development, whereby aid agencies and actors become more reflexive in shaping their roles in the dynamics of conflict; they consciously strive to 'do no harm' and potentially to be drivers for peace in addressing issues implicated in the conflict within their policies and programmes. It reflects on methodologies of conflict analysis that have become the norm by which development policy makers and practitioners guide programming priorities. In summary, it maps how ideas and practice around conflict analysis have shaped the growth of conflict and development programming in the past two decades.

Conflict analysis frameworks

Capturing the dynamic nature of conflict theories to ground the understandings of and responses to conflict is the challenge of conflict analysis in practice. Chris Mitchell's modelling of conflict analysis is one that has permeated conflict and peace studies (Mitchell 1981; Jeong 2008: 20–40; Jacoby 2008: 18–33).

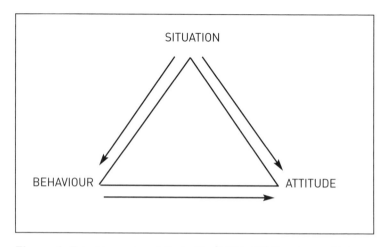

Figure 1 Triad based on Mitchell's (1981: 55) 'basic conflict structure'

Building on Galtung, he suggests a basic triad structure of conflict analysis that remains influential in conflict theory and analysis.

Defining the conflict is often itself a site of conflict for the different sides involved. For example, in the Israel/Palestine conflict the former is often said to be concerned with security while the latter is concerned with self-determination. In seeking to understand the structure of the conflict the analyst looks, for example, to explanations of the kind outlined in Chapter 2, to direct testimonies from various groups and affected populations, and to political reporting from credible sources in seeking to reach an assessment in terms of group dynamics, combat behaviour and impact on civilians. In terms of a map or matrix of conflict analysis, the researcher or analyst takes these factors and levels and digs deeper to assess the *situation* and uncover the 'issues' at stake and how entrenched or resolvable they might be. Mitchell distinguishes between issues of resources – access to water, education, land – and issues of survival, where one's identity or existence as a group or state is at stake. He defines conflict *behaviour* as 'overt actions undertaken by one party in any conflict situation, aimed at an opposing party with the intention of making that party abandon or modify its goals' (1981: 120). These can range from actions that are not openly violent – such as legislation to control minorities and limit access to housing, education and employment – to obviously violent actions such as armed attacks on members of a rival group. Group conflict *attitudes* were outlined in Chapter 2 and demonstrate how positive and negative images of self and other are created and perpetuated in fuelling conflict, and how far they need to be addressed in terms of resolving conflict.

Other well-cited applications of conflict analysis propose elements of analysis that are variations of this triad and include the following aspects: parties; goals; issues; interests; value differences; strategies for engaging with conflict; dynamics and relationships; and, above all, interventions that might be pursued to bring an end to conflict in addressing these various elements (Jeong 2008). Ramsbotham et al. (2005) propose a 'levels of analysis' approach to sources of conflict that operates at five distinctive tiers: international (global); international (regional); state (social economic, political); conflict parties (group dynamics); and elite/individual. Crocker et al. (2001) also emphasize levels of analysis in their typology of systems (systemic factors), states (state and society) and individuals (leadership and human agency). The level of conflict is important to map out: many recent wars have been termed civil wars or internal wars within state boundaries – but often they have also involved regional and global influences and impacts. Regional dynamics constitute a level of analysis that has had great attention and influence, often resulting in regional programmes. Examples include addressing small arms flows in West Africa through support to ECOWAS capacity building in this area; or promoting enhanced governance mechanisms for scarce water access and management in the

Ferghana Valley of Central Asia. Thus regional dynamics have a wider reference than simply the 'spill-over' or 'contagion' effects of war as it crosses over borders and manifests itself in the form of refugees, armed attacks on refugee camps, military incursions and border instability. They also take account of the actions of neighbours, benign and opportunistic, that can cause a conflict to erupt or escalate (Brown 2001). The imbricated relationship of Liberia and Sierra Leone in the 1990s is symptomatic of such cross-border dynamics.

The analysis of a *conflict cycle* or *stages of conflict* is another feature of the planning of interventions. Along a continuum that flows from existing sources of conflict, one may identify a stage of mobilisation and escalation (due to particular triggers, events or changes in the situation) to the point of overt violent conflict. Eventually this leads to a process of de-escalation (due to victory by one side or a successful peace process to end the violence, for example). Finally there is a period of building peace and, in the ultimate 'happy ending' scenario, reconciliation (that addresses root causes and overcomes a violent and distrustful past) among the parties (Mitchell 1981: 51; Jeong 2008: 36–7). In classic notions of intervention, the international institutional framework for peace and security shadows this continuum (escalation/overt violence/de-escalation) by evolving a continuum of responses that range from conflict prevention through to peacekeeping, peace-making and peacebuilding. While some critics rightly suggest that this is all too linear and risks being prescriptive, conflict analysts have always been at pains to stress that conflict is a dynamic process in which many factors can influence the shape and course of events. Conflicts may simmer for a long time before breaking out and may go through phases of apparent peacefulness only to re-erupt: thus the spirals, cycles and dynamics of conflict process-es can occur simultaneously or concurrently (Crocker et al. 2001: xxviii; Jeong 2008: 100–4).

For example, heightened tensions may arise from an attack by group A on group B while de-escalation efforts are under way in the form of mediated talks among the groups and a third party. This was the case in late August and early September 2010 when Israeli Prime Minister Netanyahu and President of the Palestinian Authority Mahmoud Abbas (of the PLO) were due to have talks in Washington brokered by the US government. Two violent attacks, claimed by Hamas, resulted in the death of Israeli settlers and seemed designed to increase tensions and scupper any talks. This is not just a process of inter-group conflict but also signifies another process linking the actors involved. The subtext concerns the legitimacy of Hamas, which is seen as a party to the overall Israeli/Palestinian conflict but whose legitimacy as an actor in the peace process is not accepted by Israel, the PLO or international actors who have pursued a failing policy of isolating Hamas – the elected government in Gaza – from international engagement. A range of actors are involved directly and indirectly in this conflict, with different agendas, interests and resources for conflict and peace. The issues – including sovereignty, land, security, water, and refugees – are not only inter-group but have significant interconnection with and implications for near neighbours and the region, as well as for international peace and security and wider shifts in nuclear diplomacy, anti-terrorism and the contamination of other conflict situations, notably in Iraq and Afghanistan. An accurate reading of events needs to be informed by an understanding of the conflict in all its many dimensions.

Conflict analysis in development planning

The role of conflict analysis in development has burgeoned over the past twenty years and has been instrumental in shaping the practices of conflict-sensitive development strategies and programmes adopted by many NGOs, bilateral donors and multilateral organisations. The design and purpose of conflict analysis as a tool for development in conflict and post-conflict situations is to map out the context in various ways that can inform development actors about appropriate entry points for action to promote peace and/or reduce the likelihood and incidence of conflict. Conflict-sensitive development, as discussed in earlier chapters, came to mean development actors being more engaged with conflict dynamics and context, and not simply reacting to them. Directly addressing the causes of conflict was no longer just about peacemaking and the resolution aspects but also about addressing the inequalities, weak governance, poverty and local insecurity that often underpin violence and conflict.

Conflict analysis or assessment has been developed by a range of actors to operate at both *strategic* and *programme/ project* levels. Peace and conflict impact assessment, or PCIA, is a term attributed to Kenneth Bush (1998) and emerges also from the work of various activists, including Mary Anderson at the Collaborative for Development Action, and NGOs such as Saferworld and International Alert. Bush suggests that 'PCIA is meant to empower individuals and institutions both to understand better their work, and, more importantly, to induce the changes necessary to amplify the positive impacts and to minimise negative impacts on the peace and conflict environment' (1998: 5). The methodology for strategic conflict assessment (SCA), to take another example, evolved though early path-breaking work at the UK's Department for International Development (DFID) led by Jonathan Goodhand and Tony Vaux. Many development organisations now routinely conduct such analysis with modifications to the core methodology.

Resources for conflict analysis

DFID (2002) 'Conducting Conflict Assessment: Guidance Notes', UK Department of International Development, London. http://www.dfid.gov.uk/Documents/publications/conflictassess-mentguidance.pdf

GTZ (2008) 'Peace and Conflict Assessment: a Methodological Framework for Conflict- and Peace-Oriented Alignment of Development Programmes', Gesellschaft für Technische Zusammenarbeit (GTZ) for German Federal Ministry for Economic Cooperation and Development (BMZ), Eschborn, Germany. http://www2.gtz.de/doku-mente/bib/ gtz2008-0381en-crisis-pca.pdf

NGO work on conflict sensitivity builds on a broad-based learning initiative that involved APFO (Africa Peace Forum in Kenya), CHA (Consortium of Humanitarian Agencies in Sri Lanka), CECORE (Centre for Conflict Resolution in Uganda), FEWER (Forum on Early Warning and Early Response), International Alert and Saferworld. Their collaboration resulted in a Resource Pack published in 2004: 'Conflict-Sensitive Approaches to Development, Humanitarian Assistance and Peacebuilding: a Resource Pack'. http://www.conflictsensitivity.org/publications/conflict-sensitive-approaches-development-humanitarian-assistance-and-peace-building-res

SIDA (2006) 'Manual for Conflict Analysis', Swedish International Development Assistance, Stockholm http://www.conflictsensitivity.org/sites/default/files/Manual_for_Conflict Analysis.pdf

UNDP (2003) 'Conflict-Related Development Analysis', Bureau for Crisis Prevention and Recovery, New York NY. http://www.undp.org/cpr/documents/prevention/integrate/CDA_complete.pdf

Continued

USAID (2004)'Conducting a Conflict Assessment: a Framework for Strategy and Program Development', US Agency for International Development, Washington DC.
http://www.usaid.gov/our_work/cross-cutting_programs/conflict/publications/docs/CMM_ConflAssessFrmwrk 8-17-04.pdf

Collaborative for Development Action (Boston) 'Do No Harm' Project
http://www.cdainc.com/cdawww/project_profile.php?pid=DNH&pname=Do%20No%20Harm

GSDRC: Governance and Social Development Resource Centre, a resource network established with support from UK DFID to share knowledge and tools for practitioners, including those working in conflict-sensitive development.
http://www.gsdrc.org/index.cfm?objectid=4F50B286-14C2-620A-271842F4BDFFD483#overview

---

There is convergence among types of analysis at the *strategic* level that seek to map out and understand the following elements of conflict:

- *Causes and drivers of conflict* refers to underlying trends and issues (*structural*) such as inequality and discriminatory treatment of minority groups; geographical differences in terms of quality of land and access to services; the militarisation of national government; or the presence of rich mineral resources. These causes and drivers are often analysed under the headings of political, security, social and economic factors.

- *Actors* (national, regional, international) in conflict can include governments, militias, political leaders, tribal or clan leaders, civil society organisations, human rights groups, neighbouring states, and regional or global powers; outside actors who intervene may include regional and multilateral organisations, or donors and aid organisations.

- An analysis of *dynamics and events* in recent history builds a profile of the directions of conflict and peace, and can help track the course of a conflict. Factors in play might include a new constitution, outbursts of political violence, tension in the run-up to elections, or a growing military presence in certain areas.

- This analysis of factors, actors and dynamics can help to establish the *proximate* causes of conflict – elements in the immediate environment that in some circumstances are also potential *triggers* for outbreaks of violent conflict.

- The 'do no harm' framework speaks helpfully of *dividers* and *connectors* as issues and actors that can be identified to prevent conflict deepening or even, more positively, build resources for peace.

- Based on likely triggers, possible *scenarios* (from negative to positive) can be developed for shorter- and longer-term perspectives. Such scenarios can inform planning for development programmes and also enable review and reconsideration of the existing focus of programmes.

Such analyses provide a positional snapshot of any conflict at a given time, providing a baseline for assessing interventions and projects over time and tracking progress or regression. They can help identify possible entry points for actions – political, development, security, economic and so forth. The analysis must not be static and needs to be updated frequently; its sources are continuously cross-referenced, using participatory analysis with a range of actors as well as with aid partners and beneficiaries. The DFID (UK), SIDA (Sweden), GTZ/BMZ (Germany) and UNDP are just some of the international agencies that have developed their own conflict methodologies and tools to guide aid strategy and development programming. A consortium of NGOs in 2004 developed a resource pack for conflict assessment that remains very influential and contains many similar elements. A typical conflict analysis matrix would explore in detail the issues set out below.

Table 1 Conflict analysis matrix: sample elements for a country emerging from conflict[1]

Levels of Analysis	Factors			
	Security	Political	Economic	Social
Global	Neighbouring troops have withdrawn UN Mission mandate has been extended for 6 months but peace-keepers expected to be drawn down by end of that time.	Country is on list of countries to be considered by the Peacebuilding Commission for longer-term support.	Country has been approved for HIPC debt-relief Aid dependency; volume expected to reduce and existing pledges have not been fully honoured. International business interests in timber and rubber operate through national proxies - supply lines and 'taxes' paid are unclear	Long history of migration and now subject to new EU controls

Levels of Analysis	Factors			
	Security	Political	Economic	Social
Regional/ Cross-Border	Regional organisation prepared to take up peace-keeping role Neighbouring country unstable, undermining efforts to stabilise security and border controls, including flows of arms	Good offices of regional organisation have not succeeded in preventing continued political interference of neigh-bouring President with former militias.	Cross-border trading is essential but still beset with security and corruption challenges	Flows of refugee and border camps that require massive repatriation and settle-ment programme.
National	Incomplete DDR programme Continuation and role of ex-militias as spoilers of peace agreement Integration of new national army hampered by the ineffective verifi-cation of officers and links with human rights investigations No progress on security sector reform (SSR) as government reluctant to address existing power structures in army and police	Implementation of terms of Peace Settle-ment is ongoing and precarious Continued rivalry of former rebel factions amongst politi-cal elite Weak public service with irregular payment of salaries and poor training and capacity Civil society groups emerging but weak and riven by party political affiliation	Outstanding land disputes need to be addressed through civil and traditional structures to avert conflicts as IDPs and refugees return Reliance on aid that risks distor-tions as power brokers seek access to funds to disburse to groups Political and military influence on timber and rubber industries Unmet expecta-tions a risk as it is 12 months since ceasefire and many people do not see	Over 50% of households are female-headed as a result of the war and repeated displacements There is no legislative framework for land rights and majority status for women High percentage of population under 25 with very low school enrolment rates

Levels of Analysis	Factors			
	Security	Political	Economic	Social
National (cont.)		Culture of impunity for serious human rights abuses including sexual violence	'dividends of peace' in services and functioning economy	
Local/ Sub-national	Political control of community, police and judiciary Small weapons are widely available and landmines remain a threat in more remote areas	Decentralisation of government services affected by weak and fractured central administration	Road and transport infrastructure needed to open up rural areas and access to markets for smaller farmers Tensions between IDPs and settled communities as returns accelerate following elections	Culture of violence continues as legacy of war with implication for women and children in particular Social cohesion is weak following major and multiple displacement of communities

While strategic-level conflict analysis is widely used and understood in terms of mapping out conflict causes, actors, and drivers of conflict, the practice of applying conflict analysis at the *programme* and *project* level has been more sporadic.[2] This is largely because it is very context-specific and requires an intensive hands-on process of engaging with stakeholders, project managers and beneficiaries to establish feasible parameters for peace and conflict impact analysis. It involves asking questions about particular projects and programmes and *how* they respond to the conflict situation and risk. Were they planned with the conflict or a specific fragile context in mind? What factors were considered when shaping the project? Who benefits from the project and how are benefits perceived locally? How are staffing and procurement handled and do they take account of local group dynamics and potential tensions? Has the monitoring and evaluation framework of the programme/project included ways to indicate and measure impact on conflict factors?

This engagement at the programme level involves raising awareness of staff and partners about conflict analysis and discovering to what extent considerations are implicit or absent in programmes. How might the impact on peace and conflict be better integrated into programming cycles? This involves meetings with relevant staff from the different portfolios (such as agriculture, gender, economy, community support) and with relevant partners and intended beneficiaries (communities, government, civil society organisations, other donors and international actors in the field) to consider the 'how and when' of conflict-related dynamics and factors (in design, implementation and impact analysis).

What emerges from the programme-level emphasis is the need to distinguish the particular features of indirect and direct conflict programming.

1   *Indirect conflict programming.* Development-centred programmes can become more responsive to conflict factors and risk by introducing a more explicit lens of conflict reduction into programming cycles and partnerships. For example, staff working on an education programme operating in a conflict-prone area might look more closely at the schools and communities they work with. How are they affected by the tensions around them? What role could the education programme play in ensuring it is not reinforcing divisions or empowering already powerful groups that are seeking to dominate or exclude other groups? How might schools be used to promote dialogue and interaction between communities?

2 *Direct conflict programming.* Conflict-centred activities that directly address (and seek to resolve) conflict issues can be more conscious of the risk factors in play, and aim to learn from failure as well as success in their very sensitive area of work. Let's use the example of an aid organisation working with local communities in a post-conflict setting. The aim is to establish a programme aimed at supporting the successful return of people forced to flee during the war, who now face the challenges of reintegration. The programme could be based on extensive consultations with communities to identify these challenges, and also the concerns and fears of the villagers who have remained, or even moved into property owned by displaced families. This may involve a set of projects on several fronts: to address local land disputes; to rehabilitate houses and community structures; to achieve reconciliation within and between communities; and to support agricultural development that will ensure food security for all.

In designing and measuring the impact of conflict-sensitive projects and programmes one must look through the conflict lens. This means moving beyond more conventional notions of what a successful project looks like in development terms. The impact on peace and conflict must be explicit if it is to be seen and considered in all aspects of planning, implementing and evaluating the impact of development programming in conflict-prone areas. An example from Timor-Leste is outlined in the box opposite.

The presence and absence of politics in PCIA[3]

Critical lessons have emerged from evaluations that indicate the limitations and unintended consequences of the use of conflict analysis in development strategy (Barbolet et al. 2005; Chapman

Programme level analysis: youth employment programmes in Timor-Leste

In a context where a demographic youth 'bulge' (approximately 45 per cent of the population are under 15, and 34 per cent aged 12–29) is a potential driver for conflict, claims are often made by development agencies for the conflict prevention and peacebuilding effects of supporting youth employment programmes. However, all too often these claims are not considered when measuring the impact of programmes.

For example, the International Labour Organisation (ILO) promotes youth employment in the form of road building and road repair in a number of rural districts within the 'Support for Rural Infrastructure Development and Employment Generation' initiative. A focus on outputs is the existing default measure for results. While it is helpful to know that x amount of working days were created for y amount of beneficiaries (youth, women and heads of household) over a 12-month period, and that x kilometres of road were repaired before the rainy season, this information is insufficient to confirm that the programme is addressing some key assumptions that informed the intervention – in this case, that youth unemployment and urban migration needed to be directly addressed to reduce drivers for instability and potential involvement in violence. So the extension of the impact analysis would be to look not simply at development outputs/outcomes, but to explore the extent to which the achievement of these programme outputs contributed to the reduced potential of young men in particular to engage in violence or to migrate to the capital, Dili.

This conflict-sensitive approach to impact analysis can be qualitative in using case studies and analysis based on interviews with beneficiaries, project managers, community leaders and others. Quantitative data are also available (within the usual constraints of weak systems) that can triangulate or help build a bigger picture. These include numbers of young people migrating from villages where the programme is present, numbers of jobs and new

Continued

economic activity being generated by the programme (for example, ILO staff spoke of the arrival of microlite vans as a form of rural transport along with the repaired roads providing access to markets and other benefits), and police reports on crime in the area.

Others view the ILO as doing 'cash-for-work plus', meaning that it is simply a short-term fix and a hangover from earlier humanitarian aid approaches, where communities engaged in public works in exchange for cash payments. There is a need to transition the different programme components towards addressing the structural drivers for rural economy and development – such as sustainable jobs with some status or identity – and to pursue a more strategic focus on youth that addresses social and identity issues of low status among young people – especially given the appeal of martial arts gangs and the presence of former guerrilla leaders and groups that still hold sway.

At the programme level, a social impact study is planned and its conflict impact focus will help inform the sustainability of the work schemes and the impact of the schemes on different groups, their livelihoods and their decision making about migration or work. At the strategy level, the impact study can help substantiate the claims that creating employment and other opportunities of participation in a rural economy has positive benefits for young men in Timor-Leste and reduces the risk of mobilisation for violence and conflict.

et al. 2009; DFID 2003; Hoffman 2003; OECD 2007). These include:

- The proliferation of similar approaches by different bilateral and multilateral organisations and NGOs that simply add to the existing challenge for national governments and civil society partners in developing countries to report to multiple sources; they are now asked to be involved in detailed situation analysis by multiple actors all seeking access to the same information and raising sometimes sensitive and difficult issues without commitment to following through in response to what emerges.

- Who owns the analysis? This question stresses the need for greater ownership by beneficiaries and target communities and countries of the analysis, and greater participation in identification of the actions and programmes that arise from it.

- Lack of connection between conflict analysis and programme planning, often because programme managers and local partners are not involved directly in the analysis. The assessments are often outsourced by agencies to specialists who undertake the rigorous and rich detailed analysis and then present it to the development agents and partners as a product. The buy-in of the people managing the programmes and facilitating country strategies bilaterally or under international auspices is required to ensure the analysis is not a research paper but a live information source – one that can be used not only to plan aid priorities in a conflict-sensitive manner but also to update, monitor and revise development strategies and programmes in response to shifting dynamics or events arising from the conflict itself.

- The investment of time and the costs of undertaking a comprehensive analysis often work counter to the urgency of the response needed and the real-time pressures to 'build a ship while sailing it'. Analysis tends to become a ring-fenced, lengthy event undertaken by outside experts who are often divorced from the organisational understanding and influence needed to ensure that conflict sensitivity and the understanding of 'do no harm' permeates all aspects of development financing, programming, partnerships and impact. The full assessment becomes a luxury.

- The widespread experience of conflict analysis and guidance as yet another policy trend for over-stretched development professionals in field offices has resulted in sporadic use and lack of evaluation of what is actually working.

- The reduction of conflict sensitivity to a 'tool' rather than a shift of culture, perspective and practices by aid organisations working in conflict-prone environments.
- Overemphasis on deconstructing conflict and not enough emphasis on constructing peace in terms of identifying the drivers for peace and the incentives in development programming to support and promote peaceful outcomes.

While conflict analysis frameworks focus on what could be considered structural causes of conflict or structural enablers of peace (rule of law, human rights, economic development, governance) the resulting actions tend to be short-term, stand-alone, and tied to an analysis of conflict that functions like the framed photograph caught in time rather than the film that moves, the dynamic process of engagement with conflict and change in particular settings. The common lapse and failure has not necessarily been the quality of analysis (which even academics have been willing to use and borrow) but the lack of follow-through in connecting programming and planning of aid in conflict situations with the conflict analysis process and ensuring the analysis can be timely and used, and that programming responds to it. Other, more simplified forms of support have also been developed to introduce conflict sensitivity to development planning and programmes. These include checklists to guide desk officers and programme managers in design or funding of initiatives similar to the systems developed for gender and other 'cross-cutting' issues in development. Early warning lists have been developed (by the EU and the UN, for example) that collate early warning signals and create a list of countries and situations that are regularly updated. The International Crisis Group, a think tank based in Brussels and a widely cited source of crisis information and situation analysis, maintains a 'crisis watch' on breaking situations. Not surprisingly, countries have been very reluctant to appear on such lists. At the level of new knowledge and expertise there has been a growth in specialist training of desk officers and field personnel either as one-off events or as an integrated aspect of professional training and development, measured as part of career performance. Finally, there has been a growing focus on monitoring and evaluation frameworks and the development of conflict-related indicators.

Apart from the implementation challenges of conflict analysis frameworks in development assistance policies and programmes, a wider political trend has seen the recent decline of conflict analysis as it was originally imagined. PCIA had grown from the concerns of conflict resolution academics and activists who had successfully argued that development could not remain outside of conflict and that the principle of 'do no harm' should be a minimum standard, while if possible development should seek to contribute actively to conflict reduction. The new policy trend has seen conflict analysis giving way to conflict and fragility assessments, post-conflict needs assessments, stabilisation missions, and so forth. It may be that the core elements of the analysis – the factors, actors, dynamics, and drivers of conflict – remain the same and have been reinforced by deeper assessments of security actors and capacities, trends of youth mobilisation and violence, and the role of neighbouring states: themes that reflect the current international security agenda. However, the question arises of what kinds of intervention are now being devised on the basis of these assessments. Is the purpose any longer, even in part, to 'do no harm', or is it about goals of security, stability and statebuilding that are not necessarily related to the goal of conflict reduction and resolution as understood by human security advocates of the 1980s and 1990s? These conflict and fragility assessments, notably by the OECD, DFID and the World Bank, include a wider range of issues related to governance and institutional capacities, though many similarities remain. This has left work on conflict assessment and conflict sensitivity at something of an impasse in terms of its origins in conflict resolution and the principle of 'do no harm'.

An interesting aspect of these debates is the argument by Bush (2003) that ownership of the process of analysis has to be taken by communities in conflict zones and not left to the technocratic top-down models of development agency 'tools'; in the spirit of Galtung's structural violence and positive peace, there is a call for analysis to be an act of social justice and transformation and not just a planning device. Yet development practitioners such as Gsänger and Feyen (2003) counter with the pragmatism of requiring some form of common analysis with local specificity to enable donors and partners to implement and account for projects developed in conflict zones. These debates about PCIA reflect a broader political debate about the nature and intention of peacebuilding as part of contemporary development theory, policy and practice. They reflect the resistance of grassroots and activist voices of conflict resolution and peace constituencies, who argue that their agenda for peace – centred on people and communities taking the lead in 'building' or nurturing a peace that transforms structures and relationships – has been captured and remade by an Agenda for Peace writ large, pursued by bureaucrats and international organisations (NGOs and multilaterals) with log-frames and top-down prescriptions. This argument resonates with the idea of recent international security and development operations being part of a neo-liberal agenda of spreading democracy and free markets as outlined in Chapter 1. However the middle ground suggests this is a false polarity of idealised peace and communities and demonised structures and conspiracies. The core point that needs to be acknowledged is that development assistance operating in conflict-prone areas is caught up in politics, not least in the situation on the ground but also in terms of how development actors position themselves, how aid flows impact on the situation, and how programmes are planned and implemented. As Manuela Leonhardt (2003: 58) asserts,

> An aid agency seeking to become involved in conflict resolution and peacebuilding work will not be able to avoid finding its own position within this debate. Impartiality is rarely an option. The agency's position will be largely determined by its own values and mandate, which therefore should be clearly articulated and understood among staff and other stakeholders.

Mapping out this practice of conflict and development is taken further in the next chapter in terms of the policies and debates that shape the approaches and programmes of development operations in conflict zones.

4 | The Aid Policies and Architecture of International Conflict and Development

This chapter sets out the concepts, policies and actors that have shaped the agenda and aid architecture of conflict and development, with a deliberate focus on the shaping influence of multilateral and bilateral organisations. This agenda, largely emanating from debates on donor policies, was supported by the proliferation of new multilateral and bilateral units and offices, NGOs, and private companies or consultancies that specialise in conflict, peacebuilding and post-conflict reconstruction. New knowledge and expertise alongside increased aid budgets for conflict-related programming funded interventions such as security sector reform and police training, the collection and destruction of small arms, landmine removal, and quick-impact economic and public works projects to promote peace dividends. The programmes have changed as policies have shifted to concerns of stabilisation and fragility in conflict-affected countries. Underpinning these shifts are debates about the nature of security, expressed most starkly as a stand-off between notions of human security (that tends to be more people-centred) and military security (that tends to be more state-based). These understandings of security are considered in the light of more recent trends in policy and programming that reflect shifting notions of personal, state and global security.

People, guns and soldiers: whose security and violence?

Mahbub Ul Haq, founder of the Human Development Report, shaped the measurement of well-being known as the Human Development Index that expanded the range of measures of poverty and influenced the concept of human security set out in the path-finding 1994 Report. Human security advanced a people-centred notion to counter state-centric and military conceptions:

> It means, first, safety from such chronic threats as hunger, disease and repression. And second, it means protection from sudden and hurtful disruptions in the patterns of daily life – whether in homes, in jobs or in communities. Such threats can exist at all levels of national income and development.... Human security is ... not a defensive concept – the way territorial or military security is. Instead, human security is an integrative concept.... It is embedded in a notion of solidarity among people. It cannot be brought about through force, with armies standing against armies. It can happen only if we agree that development must involve all people.... The concept of security must thus change urgently in two basic ways:
>
> • from an exclusive stress on territorial security to a much greater stress on people's security.
>
> • from security through armaments to security through sustainable human development.
>
> The list of threats to human security is long, but most can be considered under seven main categories: Economic security; Food security; Health security; Environmental security; Personal security; Community security; and Political security. (UNDP 1994: 23–4)

This understanding of human security was very influential in shaping the emerging focus on conflict prevention, positive peace, and sustainable development. It also provided impetus to arguments for 'humanitarian intervention' and the 'responsibility to protect' and underpinned a new wave of development policies and programmes directed at community security, disarmament and the effects of conflict. Activities have ranged from supporting local conflict resolution capacities, or ensuring the reintegration of former combatants, to security sector reform, small arms control, and combating sexual and gender-based violence. Critics of the 'liberal peace' such as Mark Duffield (2001; 2007) do not distinguish between human and military security *per se*, and view human security in itself as an expression of the governmentality of development and security imposed from outside and above on countries in conflict.

The events of 9/11 transformed the global security agenda and impacted upon the nature and perception of peacebuilding in particular. There followed a rapid reconfiguration of threats to security for the twenty-first century and appropriate collective responses. The hierarchy of threats emerging in Western countries in the post-9/11 world is represented clearly in the European Security Strategy (EU 2003) adopted in December 2003: terrorism, proliferation of weapons of mass destruction, regional conflicts, state failure, and organised crime. The 2005 UN World Summit reflected this difficult search for consensus on the nature of complex threats and challenges to global peace, security and development. Two key reports had been prepared: one emerged from the High-Level Panel on Threats, Challenges and Change (UN 2004) and the other in Secretary-General Kofi Annan's *In Larger Freedom: Towards Development, Security, and Human Rights for All* (UN 2005). In both reports there is broad language that speaks of protecting human rights, the insecurities of living in an interdependent world, and the essential requirement of multilateralism to meet these complex challenges. Yet, overall, they concede the shift of priorities that focuses on what some would say is a Western or Northern preoccupation with terrorism, organised crime and nuclear proliferation – and the same critics would add that this is happening at the expense of the Southern agenda, where threats are defined more broadly in terms of internal wars, HIV/AIDS, poverty, environmental degradation, and governance. It is in this context of the past two decades that we see the evolution of a continuum of conflict prevention/peace-making/peacekeeping/peacebuilding that defines the global policy environment for conflict and development.[1] Moving uneasily between the continuing search for human security and robust confrontation of new security threats, a number of concepts have guided the policies of this continuum.[2]

Humanitarian intervention

In the early 1990s humanitarian intervention emerged as a potential norm and framework for action, based on a principle of armed intervention by outside actors to guarantee the protection and human rights of citizens in states whose governments have failed to provide this protection. It was beset by ethical and practical dilemmas in its implementation, or more precisely its failures to secure these objectives. In Somalia in 1993 the operation mounted in response to war and famine floundered amid brutal media scenes of the bodies of US soldiers on the streets of Mogadishu. The failure to act in Rwanda in 1994, in the face of a genocide that resulted in the massacre of some 800,000 people over 100 days, traumatised the international community. Lessons were not learned in time for Srebrenica in 1995, where thousands of men and boys were rounded up and shot, and women were abducted and systematically raped. By Kosovo in 1999, when there was an armed intervention in the form of air strikes to protect the ethnic Albanian majority, the concept had become blurred. Justifications for the action taken were criticised as inadequately informed: NATO involvement could be seen as pre-emptive as well as triggering a humanitarian crisis. These crises prompted talk of 'new humanitarianism' informed by political awareness and proactive engagement backed by the muscle of possible military enforcement. Such a notion pulled away the veils of impartiality and neutrality that had guided humanitarian assistance. There was always an inherent tension and fear that a doctrine of humanitarian intervention would become a trapdoor to 'pre-emptive war' on questionable grounds.[3] Support for the doctrine waned as the international community became bogged down in complex emergencies and the justifications for action became caught up in shifting security debates.

However, the concept survives in part in the momentum gathered by 'responsibility to protect' (often referred to as R2P) a project spearheaded by the Government of Canada at the UN (ICISS 2001; Evans 2008). This new doctrine arose from the 2001 International Commission on Intervention and State Sovereignty and was adopted as one of the Outcomes of the 2005 World Summit at the UN. A recent UN report (2009c) provides more specificity on the terms and the responsibilities of member states in the form of 'sovereignty as responsibility'. Three pillars of action for R2P are outlined: the protective responsibilities of states; international assistance and capacity building to support that protective role; and timely and decisive responses to threats (including genocide and ethnic cleansing) through the use of means provided in the UN Charter (especially Chapter VI on pacific settlement of disputes and Chapter VIII on working with regional organisations). The report emphasises that 'no strategy for fulfilling the responsibility to protect would be complete without the possibility of collective enforcement measures, including through sanctions or coercive military action in extreme cases' (paragraph 56). This refers to the enforcement powers of Chapter VII (collective military action) that require

Security Council consensus. Sceptics and critics abound, including some UN member states who argue that R2P undermines state sovereignty. Others view such shifts as nothing more than a new balance of power run not by Realism but by Liberalism through the liberal peace (Chandler 2004).

The endurance of the debates on humanitarian interventions through R2P reflect the ongoing and indeed perennial tensions of political and moral action in relation to human rights and suffering. Does the international community respond to the primacy of states in the form of sovereignty and non-intervention in the internal affairs of states? Or does it respond as a global community with responsibility to intervene when the suffering, oppression or threat to life of citizens within a state reaches a critical point and they are not afforded the protection of their government – or when, indeed, the danger they face is emanating from that same government? This is not simply a matter of legislation or UN Security Council reform, but a necessary tension that every generation faces in defending decisions for international intervention on moral grounds. Yet as Bellamy (2009: 3) argues, even when credible guidance is available to prevent genocide and mass atrocities, 'decisions about intervention will continue to be made in an *ad hoc* fashion by political leaders balancing national interests, legal considerations, world opinion, perceived costs and humanitarian impulses – much as they were prior to R2P'. Darfur remains a ringing example of much publicity, great outrage – and limited action. Instead, Bellamy sees the impact of R2P as being the greater focus and substance given to measures for the protection of civilians and the options for action opening up beyond the impasse of doing nothing versus full-scale military intervention to prevent mass atrocities. This range of diplomatic, judicial and institutional actions, including development assistance, is found in the peacebuilding and statebuilding strategies and operations discussed in Chapter 6.

Conflict prevention

The UN Report on *Prevention of Armed Conflict* (2001) was a landmark in terms of moving from a 'culture of reaction' to a 'culture of prevention' in response to the impact of violent conflict on counties, including underdevelopment and loss of development gains, the exponential costs of peacekeeping and unwieldy Security Council mandates for such missions, and, not least, the still recent failures of humanitarian intervention. This conflict prevention framework drew on the work of the Carnegie Commission for Preventing Deadly Conflict (1997) that distinguished between *operational prevention* as 'measures applicable in the face of immediate crisis' and *structural prevention* as 'measures to ensure that crises do not arise in the first place, or if they do, that they do not recur'. The former involves addressing factors that can trigger or enable conflict – such as the availability of small arms and light weapons, unregulated exploitation of natural resources, or the prejudicial practices of 'hate' media. The latter could include support to effective institutions for governance – including the rule of law, an independent judiciary, free media, and a democratic Parliament – and addressing inequalities through economic development, support for civil society initiatives, and the promotion of education and awareness raising.

A notable implication of this approach was the need for comprehensive conflict prevention that would cut across the quite separated communities of diplomacy, human rights, and development assistance. In addressing 'root causes' of conflict, development was key, with the emphasis on addressing inequality, poverty, ethnic tensions, control of resources, and countering 'greed and grievance' motivations. Implicitly, a range of actors from national governments, regional organisations, international organisations, and civil society needed to work together. The tools of conflict prevention that were advocated included early warning systems and 'countries at risk' lists; fact-finding missions, information gathering and analysis; preventive diplomacy and good offices; preventive deployment of peacekeepers; post-conflict peacebuilding to prevent relapse into violence; and disarmament.[4] In terms of development there was a shift from working assumptions that 'all development is conflict prevention' toward 'conflict sensitivity' and 'do no harm'. Obvious challenges included the setting up of many early warning systems that produced analyses, indicators and reports without any accompanying early action. Many countries, citing concerns for sovereignty and the principle of non-interference, did not appreciate being on 'early warning' or 'at risk' lists – and as these lists became anti-terrorist lists, the concerns grew. Finally, there was the conundrum: how do you know if you have succeeded? Measuring counterfactuals in terms of what would have happened if certain actions had not been taken has proved nearly impossible, though new work on 'costs of conflict' and monitoring/evaluation is making progress in terms of justifying continued funding to conflict-related development spending and the promotion of conflict prevention (Cramer 2010; International Alert 2010; OECD 2007).

Peacebuilding

A growing mandate for peacebuilding arose, in part, from the failures of peacekeeping in the 1990s in Somalia, Rwanda and Bosnia-Herzegovina, and the resulting drive for more integrated operations that would include stronger civilian and 'soft' security aspects to shore up, consolidate and build peace on the ground. These missions, growing from the influential Brahimi Report (UN 2000) and known as 'peace support operations', refer to the new generation of peacekeeping operations that go beyond traditional mandates in which lightly armed or unarmed blue helmets are assigned to keep a peace where an agreement has already been signed and the government has invited the UN in. The Agenda for Peace had already shaken up the traditional concept by calling for 'preventive deployment' of peacekeepers as a form of conflict prevention, though Macedonia (1992–9) was the first and only clear case where this was launched successfully. The term 'peace operations' is today shorthand for a range of missions that may include peace enforcement, peacekeeping in the traditional sense, electoral observation, support to political negotiations, observing human rights, demobilisation, gender protection work, and community-based development projects. In the cases of Timor-Leste, Cambodia and Kosovo, the remit extended to setting up a 'transitional administration', whereby the UN effectively governed until an elected and stable government was in place.

Peacebuilding was initially assumed to be a *post-conflict* and post- peacekeeping activity and concern. The rise of the concept since the mid-1990s and its programmatic reach have been rapid. It is sometimes collapsed into 'nation building' or used as an umbrella for all development activities in post-conflict settings. The OECD DAC Guidelines (2001) on the role of development in conflict prevention set out the early understanding of peacebuilding emerging in conflict and development policy:

> Peacebuilding and reconciliation focus on long-term support to, and establishment of, viable political and socio-economic and cultural institutions capable of addressing the root causes of conflicts, as well as other initiatives aimed at creating the necessary conditions for sustained peace and stability. These activities also seek to promote the integration of competing or marginalised groups within mainstream society, through providing equitable access to political decision making, social networks, economic resources and information, and can be implemented in all phases of conflict. (OECD DAC 2001: 86)

Peacebuilding involves *both long-term preventive measures and more immediate responses before, during and after conflict.* It depends upon and, at the same time, seeks to foster a spirit of tolerance and reconciliation. Broad acceptance throughout society of the legitimacy of the state and the credibility of the institutions of governance is a key aspect of forging such a civic spirit.... Efforts to support participation, democratisation and peacebuilding, through strengthened institutions of governance, are clearly interlinked. (Ibid.: 113)

Interestingly, the UN did not issue a specific report or official definition – as in the examples discussed earlier – for conflict prevention and for 'responsibility to protect'. However, in 2001 the President of the UN Security Council did issue a statement on peacebuilding that employed a more operational wording of the term that includes pre- and post-conflict work.

The Security Council recognises that peacebuilding is aimed at preventing the outbreak, the recurrence or continuation of armed conflict and therefore encompasses a wide range of political, developmental, humanitarian and human rights programmes and mechanisms. This requires short- and long-term actions tailored to address the particular needs of societies sliding into conflict or emerging from it. These actions should focus on fostering sustainable institutions and processes in areas such as sustainable development, the eradication of poverty and inequalities, transparent and accountable governance, the promotion of democracy, respect for human rights and the rule of law and the promotion of a culture of peace and non-violence.... [T]he Council underlines that international efforts in peacebuilding must complement and not supplant the essential role of the country concerned. (Security Council, 20 February 2001, Statement of the President of the Security Council, S/ PRST/2001/5)

Peacebuilding as concept, policy and programming lent impetus to the establishment of the UN Peacebuilding Commission

(PBC) in 2005 as one of the significant outcomes of the 2005 World Summit.⁵ It was burdened with the expectation of improving international responses to an increasing number of complex, insecure and protracted conflicts. The relapse into violent conflict in countries where peace agreements have been brokered and benchmarks such as elections have been satisfied served to reinforce the long-term political and financial commitment required to build lasting peace. The mandate of the Commission included the bringing together of relevant actors to 'propose integrated strategies for post-conflict peacebuilding and recovery', encourage 'focus on reconstruction and institution-building efforts', help 'improve coordination of all relevant actors within and outside the United Nations system', address 'predictable financing for early recovery activities', and 'extend the period of attention given by the international community to post-conflict recovery'.⁶ Burundi, Sierra Leone, Guinea-Bissau and the Central African Republic have been the focus for the Commission's work, with very mixed results.

Challenges have ensued, including the question of whether the lack of action can be resolved through the creation of another international body, or whether it is a matter of field coordination and focus. Also at issue is the competition for donor resources and whether the Peacebuilding Fund simply diverts monies that may have gone through other programmes and channels to the countries concerned. Given the inter-governmental nature of the Commission, the question is also raised of how likely members are to challenge government priorities and actions, particularly in situations where governments might be part of the problem rather than the solution (UN 2010a; Atwood and Tanner 2007). A review of the UN peacebuilding architecture in 2010 was co-facilitated by three member-state ambassadors, involving a process of wider consultation within and outside the UN. It is direct in its conclusion that 'either there is a conscious recommitment to peacebuilding at the very heart of the work of the United Nations, or the Peacebuilding Commission settles into the limited role that has developed so far' (UN 2010a). One of the main themes emerging from the review is the precise relationship of development to peacebuilding, given the failures of peacebuilding strategies to deliver basic development needs in some post-conflict settings.

Civil society actors remain critical of the limited role they have been given in the planning and work of the Commission. There are also very real tensions about how the original grassroots project of peacebuilding initiatives – defined as local and community-based efforts to build peace – has been expanded and even 'hijacked' to cover the present full range of post-conflict development and recovery activities that scale up to multi-million dollar operations. This theme is taken up in Chapter 6.

Fragile states, stability and statebuilding

The terminology of 'fragile' or 'failed' states became more prominent in defining the post-9/11 world of new threats and the 'war on terror'.[7] This parameter of the new global policy environment led to a certain growing acceptability of the term to refer to chronic and acute crises of governance, security and poverty that lead to high levels of lawlessness and ungovernability, increasingly linked to fears of 'safe havens' and 'breeding grounds' for terrorism. That fragile states create an enabling environment for non-state groups with criminal and militarised resources to consolidate power is now a major concern of much of the discourse and policies underpinning Western notions of security and development. This risks making 'development' hostage to military and security concerns as underdevelopment itself is conceived as a security threat.

The OECD's Development Assistance Committee (OECD DAC) set out, in collaboration with donors, the 'Principles for Good International Engagement in Fragile States and Situations' in 2007 and has issued more recent reports on statebuilding (2008; 2010a). It also convened the process which led to the Dili Declaration by the International Dialogue on Peacebuilding and Statebuilding (2010). The OECD's *Principles* include, inter alia, 'do no harm'; anti-corruption efforts; linking political, security and development objectives; improved and shared context analysis; avoiding pockets of exclusion; and remaining engaged over longer timeframes. The DAC understanding of fragility is closely tied to a process of state formation and building based on the classic Western tradition of the social contract:

> [F]ragility arises primarily from weaknesses in the dynamic polit-ical process through which citizens' expectations of the state and state expectations of citizens are reconciled and brought into equi-librium with the state's capacity to deliver services. Reaching equi-librium in this negotiation over the social contract is the critical if not sole determinant of resilience, and disequilibrium the determi-nant of fragility. Disequilibrium can arise as a result of extremes of incapacity, élite behaviour, or crises of legitimacy. It can arise through shocks or chronic erosion and can be driven alternately by internal and external factors. (OECD DAC 2008: 7)

> Statebuilding is seen as the response to fragility ... in the broader context of state-formation processes and state–society relations. [It is] a primarily endogenous development founded on a political process of negotiation and contestation between the state and societal groups. (Ibid.: 3)

The focus is on the state's ability to provide services to its citizens and for citizens in their turn to be able to demand such services and hold the state accountable. Security is clearly defined as one such service in conflict-prone environments. This approach indicates nothing less than the transformation of the core culture of development theory and practice from one of addressing poverty to one of addressing state fragility:

> a focus on statebuilding, if understood as support for the state–society contract and its gradual institutionalisation, is equally, if not more, important than poverty reduction as a framework for engagement. This is particularly true in divided or post-war states, where poverty reduction remains a goal but is perhaps not the most appropriate overall framework for engagement. Rather, overall state-building strategy processes should frame, and not replace, post-conflict needs assessment (PCNA) and poverty reduction strategy paper (PRSP) mechanisms. (Ibid.: 8)

Such a shift in policy focus goes to the heart of the tensions of politicising development aid that concern many observers and indeed practitioners. While political concerns are not new – and indeed the growing governance agenda has been part of development discourse and practice throughout[8] – the new articulations of fragility and stability propose a fundamental rethinking of the ethics and objectives of development aid in conflict zones.

DFID,[9] in its 2009 government White Paper, set out a specific section on 'Building Peaceful States and Society' that promoted 'working across government' in what is known as the 'whole of government approach'. This brought defence, development and diplomacy together in working on a priority list of at-risk or fragile states; a commitment was made that 50 per cent of new bilateral assistance would be to fragile countries. The theme was taken up in 2010 in a 'practice paper' issued by DFID under the same title that drew heavily on the DAC approach of state–society relations – though the diffusion of norms is as likely to have flowed from UK policy to DAC policy.

> Statebuilding is concerned with the state's capacity, institutions and legitimacy, and with the political and economic processes that

underpin state–society relations. The effectiveness of the state and the quality of its linkages to society largely determine a country's prospects for peace and development.... Statebuilding is a long-term, historically rooted and internal process driven by a wide range of local and national actors. In fragile contexts it often reveals tensions between state and non-state actors, with each wanting to exert influence and establish a dominant position. (DFID 2010: 12)

Somewhat surprising (and it will be interesting to see this in practice) is the commitment in the paper to Galtung's understanding of positive peace, outlined in Chapter 2. This goes beyond the absence of violence and seeks to address 'structural' aspects of conflict such as human rights, exclusion and poverty. The DFID practice paper states that peacebuilding 'aims to establish positive peace ... supported by political institutions that are able to manage change and resolve disputes without resorting to violent conflict'. On this basis DFID outlines an integrated framework for statebuilding and peacebuilding in situations of conflict and fragility: 'address the causes and effects of conflict and fragility, and build conflict resolution mechanisms'; 'support inclusive political settlements and processes'; 'develop core state functions' (including security); and 'respond to public expectations' (referring to the ability to enable state–society negotiation of priorities and needs).

These concepts and understandings of fragile states and of statebuilding as peacebuilding have become the staple of recent international development programmes among many donors and influence the shape of ongoing UN peace operations.

Conflict and development programmes

In the shift from human security to the security–development nexus, the ideas and programmes of security supported by development aid have been contested. The development of modular programmes – whereby there are pre-designed approaches to a range of interventions including security sector reform (SSR), disarmament, demobilisation and reintegration (DDR), control of access to small arms and light weapons (SALW), and employment creation – has led to some concern about 'one size fits all' approaches that are transplanted from one context to another. The range of programmes now being implemented as part of core development budgets is wide:

- support to peace processes and the implementation of peace agreements;
- electoral support and institution building for parties and parliaments;
- quick-impact projects to support fragile peace, create opportunities to revitalise economic incomes, and generate safer livelihoods;
- small arms reduction and mine action;
- civilian aspects of policing and broader security sector reform;
- reintegration of IDPs and demobilised combatants;
- strengthening governance and the rule of law, including access to justice, arbitration, grievance mechanisms and human rights and truth commissions;
- DDR processes;
- strengthening of civil society and state–civil society initiatives for dialogue.

The evolution of 'security and governance' projects and approaches was the strongest indication of how far a new conflict and development agenda was emerging and changing the way development and change were being managed in conflict-affected countries.

The shift from small arms and light weapons to armed violence reduction

Concern about weapons of war often focuses on the role of advanced technology, particularly in moving to high-precision, distant killing. Yet in many wars it is small arms, a flourishing second-hand global market and illegal trafficking that fuel destructive conflict. A UN conference in 2001 provided momentum on SALW by creating a global commitment to more transparency in these notoriously opaque trade and supply chains. This resulted in a UN Programme of Action to Prevent, Combat and Eradicate the Illicit Trade in Small Arms and Light Weapons in All Its Aspects. Implementation has been slow but signs of progress include the development of regional initiatives to control illicit flows of arms. Examples are the 2004 Nairobi Protocol for the Prevention, Control and Reduction of Small Arms and Light Weapons, which applies to countries in the Great Lakes region and the Horn of Africa, and the 2006 ECOWAS Convention on Small Arms and Light Weapons, Their Ammunition, and other Related Materials. Since 2006 the UN has been working on (but is still a long way from tabling) a global arms trade treaty dealing with conventional arms.

Programmes and projects in small arms reduction flourished and took the form of high-visibility collection and destruction programmes, sometimes including cash payments or other incentives for ex-combatants and civilians to turn in arms. Such projects sometimes link up with DDR programmes. The focus on SALW, like many trends in international action, had waned somewhat by the second half of the past decade, partly reflecting doubts about the sustainability of such projects and the perverse incentives created. For example, anecdotes abounded of people burying the 'good' guns and trading in the poorer-quality weapons for cash. Nonetheless, there is consensus that the availability of cheap small arms and light weapons continues to be a driver of conflict and violence.

The agenda for SALW has been reinvented and some would say reinvigorated by the promotion of a broader community security approach referred to as armed violence reduction (AVR). At the global level this has been expressed through the Geneva Declaration on Armed Violence and Development endorsed by over 100 states since 2006. This platform advocates a greater role for development in reducing the threat and reality of armed violence in all its forms – conflict-related, crime-related, interpersonal. The argument made is that such violence is an impediment to achieving the MDGs.

Recent debate and thinking have focused on the role of community security – and the need to counter armed force that includes criminal and domestic violence, for example – in promoting locally owned and sustainable programmes of reducing conflict. For example, lessons are being drawn from innovative work on urban violence and drug-related crime in Latin America, and applied to war situations in Africa, where understandings of violence have tended to be framed in limited notions of warring parties and groups. AVR focuses on the interlinkages of crime and conflict violence in many settings, on youth programming to target those vulnerable to violence and vulnerable to being brought into cultures of violence, and on cities and urban settings. A recent report by the World Bank (2010: ix) on urban violence finds that '[i]n many cases, the scale of urban violence can eclipse that of open warfare. Some of the world's highest homicide rates occur in countries that have not undergone wars but have violence epidemics in their urban areas.' AVR also returns to human security roots in advocating community self-understanding of security and leadership in responses. The tools used include community surveys and dialogues, and the establishment of committees and relations with municipalities, local police and other groups.

Sources: OECD (2009); Oxfam, IANSA and Saferworld (2007); World Bank (2010); Geneva Declaration at http://www.genevadeclaration.org/

One feature of the rise of armed violence reduction (AVR, see box above) is the expectation that it will usher in a second generation of SSR programmes that will be bottom-up as well as top-down. The design elements are a combination of well-established military training and cooperation initiatives and governance-based policy development that links the institutions of security with civilian control and oversight – notably through parliamentary and civil society involvement in the accountability of the army, police, and border guards, and through overall budgets for security and defence spending. For example, the OECD DAC issued guidance on security sector reform and governance in 2004.[9] While policy guidelines and concepts for intended interventions are quite sophisticated, the practice of SSR has been more sporadic. Criticism has concentrated on the dominance of military expertise, even in so-called multi-disciplinary teams; the failure to develop civilian skills and approaches; and the need to link the very top-down and stand-alone approach to SSR more directly to bottom-up and community security concerns. The role of national security interests is also a factor in this area: it is not unusual in very volatile settings to find a series of bilateral security sector cooperation arrangements operating alongside (and sometimes undermining) UN-mandated missions seeking to establish commitments with emerging governments on the vetting of officers and the pursuit of force members answerable for human rights and other abuses. Timor-Leste and the Democratic Republic of Congo are just two examples.

New agendas of conflict, security and development: climate change, insecurity and conflict

More recently the complex global challenges posed by the environmental agendas of scarce resources and climate change have emerged as future drivers of conflict (Homer-Dixon 1994; Gleditsch 1998; Mazo 2010). However, even if research is beginning to target the relationship between environmental security and conflict, policy responses (never mind consensus on the

Climate change, natural resources and conflict

The Mekong River Basin encloses areas of Lao PDR, Thailand, Viet Nam and Cambodia. It is a vulnerable, low-lying coastal area facing rising sea levels as a consequence of climate change and associated problems of future flooding, as well as drought related to reduced rainfall. The Mekong River Commission was established in 1995 by the four countries, with support from a range of international aid donors including Australia, Sweden and Germany. It provides a governance and cooperation framework for an integrated water management strategy. This includes a focus on climate change and adaptation, and so development assistance is supporting technical research and testing to examine scenarios for climate change and impacts on displacement, livelihoods, and economy to inform preventive and sustainable solutions.

The Nile Basin Initiative, established in 1999, emerged from upstream and downstream tensions concerning access to and use of the river – in particular the relative dominance of Egyptian control of the resource despite the fact that other countries (notably Burundi, Democratic Republic of Congo, Ethiopia, Kenya, Rwanda, Sudan, Tanzania and Uganda) rely on the river for water, energy and economic impact. The Initiative has provided a framework for negotiating a long-term Commission to address access, security, irrigation, climate change, and development challenges on a sustainable footing. In 2010 this took a significant step forward: a Common Framework Agreement, debated and negotiated over some time, has been signed by some of the members. Despite some reservations on the part of Sudan and Egypt, and concern about the role of the international financial institutions, it is anticipated that a new phase in regional cooperation and integration is about to begin.

This initiative is funded in part by the members themselves, with international support from a host of international donors including the World Bank, the UN, the UK, Norway and others. The UK has also funded the Nile Basin Dialogue, a forum for civil society engagement among all members of the communities and groups affected by the issues and intended beneficiaries of the many projects managed through the initiative. *Sources*: http://www.nilebasin.org/ (accessed 12 October 2010); http://www.mrcmekong.org/programmes/bdp.htm (accessed 15 December 2010)

problem) remain few and fledgling (Smith and Vivekananda 2009; Buhaug, Gleditsch and Theisen 2008). In practice, one thus finds projects and programmes aimed at addressing resource conflicts under the rubric of conflict prevention and peacebuilding.

There is a need for more grounded mapping and analysis of local factors of conflict and how they interact, and this is starting to happen (Saferworld 2009). As stressed in Chapter 2, no one factor on its own (access to natural resources, poverty, ethnic and identity politics, poor growth, inequality, et cetera) can be said to cause conflict. In Darfur, for example, the added tensions of pastoralists and farmers as a local conflict over resources and the impact of environmental degradation have been drivers of the killings and conflicts, but cannot be said to have determined them. There is consensus that climate change cannot be the only factor or risk promoting conflict, and therefore no causal relationship can be presumed. Climate change on its own will not cause wars – but it can be a 'threat multiplier' or cause 'consequences of consequence' such that conditions of weak states, low resilience in communities, and poor adaptation to a shifting water table, desertification and soil erosion patterns all combine in possible permutations to fuel the risk of conflict and insecurity (Mazo 2010; Smith and Vivekananda 2009).

Organisational developments

This changing global policy environment has been accompanied by a proliferation of actors, as many organisations reposition themselves within the changing global context. For example, the UN is no longer the only, or necessarily the leading, provider of peacekeeping. We have witnessed a growing role for regional organisations, most particularly the AU, in African peace and security. The hybrid AU/UN mission (UNAMID) in Darfur is the weightiest of these AU mission commitments, though it is also active in Burundi and Somalia. At the same time, NATO has reconfigured itself – formerly a Cold War alliance – to take on wider peacekeeping and stabilisation tasks, as seen in its leadership of the International Security Assistace Force (ISAF) in Afghanistan and non-combat military training in Iraq. The EU continues to build its military and civilian capacities for crisis management, and is undertaking a number of missions in its near neighbourhood (Kosovo) as well as further afield (DRC, Georgia). These include border management, police training and rule-of-law interventions. While many of the missions are UN-mandated, there is a rise in EU-led missions. As a result of these policy developments, ways of working in and on conflict have evolved very rapidly.

Dedicated units working on conflict and crisis issues are now a feature of multilateral and bilateral aid institutions, including the Conflict, Humanitarian and Security Department (CHASE) in the Department for International Development (DFID) in the UK, the Conflict Prevention and Crisis Management unit in the European Commission, the Bureau for Crisis Prevention and Recovery in UNDP, the Conflict Unit at the World Bank, and the Network on Conflict Prevention and Development cooperation at the OECD DAC. In the UK these organisational adaptations to changing national security considerations and to the changed global policy environment for working on conflict can be seen in the transitions of the Post-Conflict Reconstruction Unit to a Stabilisation Unit, with the continued existence of the Conflict Prevention Pool – another cross-government entity that in itself has undergone changes of focus and strategy in seeking to define actions for conflict prevention in a context where Afghanistan in particular is a major focus for UK military and aid commitments. These units are all cross-government, including participation by the Ministry of Defence (MOD), the Foreign and Commonwealth Office (FCO), and DFID.

Specialised civil society organisations have also proliferated in the form of NGOs and think tanks, including the African Centre for Constructive Resolution of Disputes (ACCORD), the International Crisis Group (ICG), the Centre for Humanitarian Dialogue (CHD), International Alert, Interpeace, the European Peacebuilding Liaison Office, Saferworld, and the West Africa Network for Peace (WANEP). One estimate suggests that INGOs in the wider field of humanitarian and development assistance grew from 1,083 in 1914 to 37,000 in 2000; nearly 20 per cent of these INGOs were formed after 1990 (UNDP 2002). Global deployment of humanitarian field staff has increased annually by an average of 6 per cent during the past decade; there are now estimated to be some 210,800 humanitarian aid workers with accredited organisations (ALNAP 2010). As noted above, regional organisations like the AU have also taken on new roles and prominence in peace and security issues. In 2004 the AU established its Peace and Security Council (with a Secretariat) to consider continent-wide security issues, and it is building up capacity in the areas of peacekeeping, peacebuilding and media-tion (peacemaking). Since 2007 this Council has held annual con-sultations with the UN Security Council and works with the UN in peace operations in Darfur, as mentioned earlier. In Somalia, the AU leads a UN-mandated peacekeeping mission (AMISOM); it also has a Peace and Security Partnership with the EU under the joint Africa-EU strategy to strengthen the Africa Peace and Security Architecture (APSA).

New funding mechanisms have been developed to facilitate rapid response and flexibility outside of normal development funding cycles. In 2007 the European Commission's Rapid Reaction Mechanism (2001) was folded into the much larger Instrument for Stability. The Conflict Prevention Pools established by the UK government in 2001 involve the FCO, the MOD and DFID in regional and thematic initiatives. The UN Action Multi-Donor Trust Fund was established in 2008 to combat sexual violence in conflict. In terms of the global expertise and experience now available in a range of fields, updated staffing profiles include conflict advisers and specialists in transitional justice, security sector reform and civil–military relations.

When it comes to development assistance in conflict-related settings, the forum of the OECD DAC (with 79 member states) has been at the forefront of developing international policy norms and practices for donors. In 1997 it formulated the 'DAC Guidelines on Conflict, Peace and Development Cooperation on the Threshold of the Twenty-First Century', now referred to simply as the 'DAC Guidelines' (OECD DAC 1998). These definitions and debates on conflict prevention, security sector reform and post-conflict governance have shaped the nature of development assistance to conflict situations. The OECD DAC established a network on Fragile States parallel to a pre-existing and successful network on Conflict Prevention and Development Cooperation that shaped the DAC Guidelines. Indeed the coexistence and interaction of these two networks reflected the double-handed international response to conflict and security threats that was evolving. Their merging in 2008 into the new network on International Conflict and Fragility (INCAF) reflects the convergence of policy and practice from conflict prevention and peacebuilding to take on more explicitly the implications of fragility and statebuilding. This echoed other donor actions, notably in 2007 when the World Bank prioritised 'fragile and conflict-affected countries' as one of its six strategic themes and replaced previous funding mechanisms with the new State- and Peacebuilding Fund. The OECD DAC has kept pace with and sometimes led the way in the shifting security and development policy debates of the 2000s. It has guided donor funding, policy and practice in the areas of conflict prevention, security sector reform and statebuilding in the context of fragile states.

On a more technical level the OECD is the repository for aid statistics and the coding of aid, which has become a very important issue. If spending is coded as 'ODA-eligible' – that is, it can be classified as development aid – then it counts toward the 0.7 per cent of gross national income (GNI) that has been set as an international target for donor-country governments. In 2004 and 2005 new codes for conflict-related programming were added to the ODA list to include: (1) support to civilian peacebuilding and conflict prevention/resolution by such means as information exchange, dialogue and capacity building; (2) small arms and light weapons collection and destruction (not stockpiling); (3) technical assistance on the civilian side of SSR, including police, border management, parliamentary oversight of defence budgets, and reform of defence ministries as part of wider SSR; (4) preventing recruitment of child soldiers and assisting in their demobilisation; and (5) participation in and support to UN peacebuilding operations. Strict peacekeeping remains controversial, though associated costs of peacekeeping can be ODA-eligible if carried out by a country's own troops as part of a UN mission.

As a result of these policy and organisational developments, ways of working have changed profoundly for development actors in conflict zones around the world. New partnerships have emerged where diplomacy, defence and development specialists are encouraged to work more closely – the challenge of working across government and organisations in what is termed the 'whole of government' approach. Partnerships with civil society reflect in part the heightened tensions of 'implementing partner' versus 'independent critic' which has always framed this relationship. There is also a new tension among development NGOs and specialised peacebuilding NGOs in terms of trade-offs and compromise between poverty and impartiality versus peace and security priorities. These new ways of working and the inherent tensions within them reflect the underlying tensions of human and military security that have framed the role of development in conflict situations over the past two decades. They lie at the heart of the dilemmas of statebuilding and peacebuilding as the apotheosis of the post-Cold War conflict and development agenda. This double-handed strategy of peacebuilding/statebuilding has emerged as the dominant policy discourse for engaging with so-called 'fragile states'. There is little doubt that both the exceptional cases of Iraq and Afghanistan are driving changes in the understanding and practice of peacebuilding and statebuilding, with significant challenges and dilemmas for the role of international development. These dilemmas are the focus of Chapter 6.

5 | Women, Peace and Security: the Gendering of International Conflict and Development

In many states, war came to women, children and non-combatant men. They were frequently direct and indirect casualties of the fighting, targets for torture, maiming and murder, victims of starvation and siege, or forced relocation and forced labour. Women and young people were often agents in occupied or fighting zones, as fighters or supporters, and some as collaborators or unwilling hostages. Their experiences of violence and strategies for resistance and survival are told more often in books and films than in the IR [International Relations] literature. Forgetting these experiences is forced as part of the 'normalisation' process, but also brought about by discomfort in the face of moral dilemmas about complicity and choice, responsibility and blame. (Jan Jindy Pettman in *Worlding Women*, 1996: 129)

Often, it is the assumptions that women are born peace-lovers, care-givers and nurturers that have placed a disproportionately heavy burden on women's NGOs all over the world. From Palestine to Kosovo to Rwanda, women's NGOs have increasingly been targeted by international agencies and Western donors as those who should and could bring about peace and reconciliation to the warring parties, a formidable task even for the best organized, financed, and supported national and international institutions. Equally, women's NGOs are often expected by national governments and international NGOs to take care of victims of violence and refugees by their own strengths and resources, while national and international money goes elsewhere. And still, when it comes to decision making women's voices are more than regularly ignored by these same national and international institutions and agencies, and voices of government officials and warlords are listened to, instead. (Dubravka Zarkov in the Foreword to *Gender, Violent Conflict and Development,* 2008)

This chapter explores gender as an early and continuing theme of the relationship between conflict and development. And it considers some flow patterns in the current political momentum surrounding women, peace and security internationally. As the opening quotations show, the struggles of gender, conflict and development have been in part about people and institutions. The academic investigation of gender and war has been enriched by theoretical and field work undertaken by a generation of activists, researchers and academics, notably in the sub-disciplines and literatures of Gender and Development and Feminist International Relations. Gender and Development has a long history embracing the ground-breaking work of Ester Boserup (1970) on the role of women in economic development around the world and many thinkers and activists who elaborated feminist frameworks for understanding women as agents and subjects of development, in as many settings.[1]

The core aspects of these frameworks can be summarised here. The gender dimensions of the roles that women play in economic development have been made visible in work settings that are both productive (as farmers, traders, workers) and reproductive (as mothers, family carers and community workers). Their public and private spaces have been delineated, along with the structures within which gender relations operate – whether household, clan and kinship, or political structures. Theorists and activists have built a rights-based approach to gender and development whereby 'women's rights as human rights' is a matter not only of gender equality but of gender justice. By positioning women as 'subjects' of development theory, policy and practice, the challenges of culture, class, ethnicity and other forms of identity in the analysis of gender relations and structures have been addressed. And strategic responses have explored how women are 'targeted' versus how gender is 'mainstreamed' into development planning and programmes. Any and all of these themes are subject to keen internal debate within development studies and within feminist, gender and women's studies. It is this contestation that enables feminist research and analysis to remain a self-critical entry to discourses and practices of international development, including in the field of post-war reconstruction. While humanitarian development and post-conflict development as well as peacebuilding have featured in gender and development debates – and indeed some theorists cut across a range of disciplines and so defy categorisation under development studies, economics, law, politics or international relations – it is to feminist International Relations (IR) that we can look for some of the foundational work on women and war in particular.

A first task of feminist IR was to render women visible in the concerns of states, security, and institutions that were the mainstream of the discipline.[2] In looking to war and peace, feminist IR research uncovered and debated both the implicit roles and norms attributed to women as well as the systemic workings of militarism and pacifism and their gendering of war and peace.[3] More recent works on women and war range across themes that include the enduring fascination with 'roles' and 'aberrations', such as the female suicide bombers of Palestine and other perpetrators of violence;[4] the new structural and systemic workings of patriarchy and militarism in the context of the global 'war on terror';[5] and the assiduous documentation of women's civil society activism and grassroots work for peace.[6] In addition, there is a growing and credible body of policy and advocacy work that shapes and is shaped by the context of a new generation of

international aid, security and post-conflict development operations worldwide, involving a varied host of actors from women's
community groups to Special Representatives and Envoys.[7]

Mary Burguieres (1990) provides a helpful distinction between
roles and *systems* that captures the range of feminist analytical
approaches in the women and war literature. She outlines three
schools of thought for feminist analysis of peace and war. The
first school embraces and amplifies the maternal female stereotype as the basis of a peaceful society. The second school rejects
the pacific female stereotype and argues that women perform
military roles in defence of the state as capably as men. The third
school goes beyond the representations of roles and points instead
to formative operations of structural power in the promotion of
militarism; militarism and patriarchy as operations of power are
seen as mutually reinforcing in the subordination of women and
femininity and the valorisation of men and masculinity.

Understanding gender as role-playing

Early feminist focus on women and war anticipated the transformative potential of anti-colonial wars for women in Africa, Asia
and Latin America. However, when country after country yielded
a post-revolutionary reality of women being ushered back into
their households, the romantic appeal of liberating women
through liberating states lost its lustre.[8] Cynthia Enloe (1988) and
Christine Sylvester (1987) emphasise the taking up of unconven-
tional roles by women and the politicisation of traditional gender
roles as cause for optimism stemming from women's participation in those wars. Women fighters receive particular attention as
subversives who transform the expectations of male–female
gender relations in the course of revolutions. Sylvester suggests
that the woman warrior identity is one that can be mobilised to

anti-patriarchal ends as it overturns existing gendered divisions of labour and social power relations. But such changes, it would seem, are mere suspensions of ingrained 'normality'; revolutionaries become statesmen and so in the aftermath of revolution women find themselves back in the private domain of the household.

The categories of participation open to women in war are tied to an operation of patriarchal power that depends on a 'presence/absence' dynamic whereby a set of male values are valorised in opposition to devalued female 'others'. This dynamic means that 'the presence of men depends on the absence of women. Because of this interdependence, a gender analysis of women's lives and experiences does not simply "add something" about women but *transforms* what we know about *men* and the activities they undertake' (emphases in original) (Peterson and Runyan 1993: 7–8). This defines a public and private space where society sets sanctions and rewards for women's aberrant actions during war. Susan Brownmiller (1976) and Enloe (1988) argue that, as a result, women are more readily positioned in non-combat, supporting roles as wives, defence workers, nurses, drivers, administrators and prostitutes; they are the camp followers. Even in the archetypal male role of fighter, women must be constructed in such a way as to perpetuate male power and female subordination in this gendered process of militarisation. Enloe (2002) also suggests that the aberrations and expectations of women's work under militarisation are not confined to state militaries. Irregular armies such as guerrilla forces recruit women not simply to transform their social and political position but also, like state armies, to optimise the military effectiveness of insurgent operations. This involves allocating roles according to gender, generation and marital status that often perpetuate power-inscribed divisions of labour. To that extent the gendered processes of militarisation, predicated on particular understandings of masculinity and femininity formalised in state militaries, also find meaning in non-state forces.

By revealing such gendered assumptions within militarism as ideology, feminists have sought to subvert them. Jean Bethke Elshtain in *Women and War* subverts the life-giving/life-taking, male/female axes that reinforce militarism as gendered power relations. In their stead she coins some new categories of female identities: Ferocious Few, Non-Combatant Many and Aggressive Mother. Male identities are extended to include Militant Many, Pacific Few, and Compassionate Warriors. These point to a more fluid and complex reading of gender roles in war and peace. The artificiality of gendered public and private space constructed through militarisation is further challenged by Enloe (1988) when she highlights the paradox of women as nurses, soldiers, intelligence workers and prostitutes, located close to the front-line but still viewed as 'homefront' participants. As Pettman argues, the victim, vulnerable, protected identity has to be paid for by silence, acquiescence and the loss of an acting self that deprives women of agency. Such an explanation of women's relationship to war, she argues, 'de-politicises their actions, and makes their agency or politics appear unruly, rebellious, ungrateful or asking for trouble' (1996: 99–100). There is tension, therefore, in the balance between seeing women as perpetual victims of violence or as transformed through participation in violent conflict. Neither extreme empowers or reflects the experiences of many women caught up in war. The challenge is to balance a representation of women's struggles that neither perpetuates them as victims nor seeks to stereotype their activities as tied to particular roles.

The persistence of notions of fixed roles in war and peace is found even in the exceptionalism of particular gender identities for women. Laura Sjoberg and Caroline Gentry (2007) explore the representations and agency of women who commit violence that is considered beyond acceptable norms; women who are, by exception, suicide bombers in the Middle East and Chechnya, and genocidaires in Bosnia-Herzegovina and Rwanda. They argue that the treatment of such women in media coverage and political debate (and in some feminist analyses) as deviant, aberrations, and somehow exceptional and inhuman, only serves to underscore the persistence of traditional gendered stereotypes and assumptions in the global politics of war and peace. These stereotypes persist in subordinating the agency of women as political actors by viewing extreme actions as thwarted femininity, hypersexuality, or plain old irrationality and madness rather than involving some degree of choice or rationality.

Moving from gender roles to gender transformations

Maxine Molyneux (1985) speaks, in the context of revolutionary Nicaragua, of 'mobilisation without emancipation' for women and makes a very powerful distinction between what she terms 'strategic' and 'practical' gender interests. This theory of interests has been very influential in shaping understandings of gender, power and transformation in feminist approaches to development theory and practice as well as political participation. Strategic gender interests (in this case for women) are directed at an overarching transformation of women's environment in ways that address power imbalances based on analysis and involving a politicised feminist consciousness in doing so.

> Strategic interests are derived in the first instance deductively, that is, from the analysis of women's subordination and from the formulation of an alternative, more satisfactory set of arrangements to those which exist. These ethical and theoretical criteria assist in the formulation of strategic objectives to overcome women's subordination, such as the abolition of the sexual division of labour,

the alleviation of the burden of domestic labour and childcare, the removal of institutionalised forms of discrimination, the attainment of political equality, the establishment of freedom of choice over childbearing, and the adoption of adequate measures against male violence and control over women. (Ibid.: 232–3)

Practical gender interests focus on the immediate contextual interest, based on where a woman might be positioned, and are aimed at improving access to resources and services within a prevailing gendered set-up – and not necessarily at transforming it.

Practical gender interests are given inductively and arise from the concrete conditions of women's positioning within the gender division of labour. In contrast to strategic gender interests, these are formulated by the women who are themselves within these positions rather than through external interventions. Practical interests are usually a response to an immediate perceived need, and they do not generally entail a strategic goal such as women's emancipation or gender equality. (Ibid.: 233)

These interests find expression in collective actions in the face of hardship and strife – for example, food riots or demonstrations against government policies – but 'do not in themselves challenge the prevailing forms of gender subordination, even though they arise directly out of them' (ibid.: 233). The conceptualisation of strategic and practical gender interests has been taken up by Caroline Moser (1991) in the context of development planning, where she speaks of practical and strategic gender 'needs' rather than interests. This is criticised by Naila Kabeer (1994), who sees the shift from interests to needs as removing the political imperative of gender as power. The debate remains very relevant to contemporary conflict and current debates on the state of gender analysis and development planning, not least in respect of women caught up in humanitarian aid systems and in statebuilding and peacebuilding processes in post-conflict settings.

Molyneux uses her strategic/practical distinction to explain that revolutionary war in Nicaragua failed to liberate women because nationalism subsumed women's struggles, preventing the emergence of a feminist consciousness that could give transformative meaning and effect to women's participation. Because for many liberation movements the primary site of oppression is held to be national identity, any focus on women's struggles to transform gender relations is interpreted as undermining the wider struggle. Women, therefore, are viewed as a political constituency to be mobilised for support in the same way as other sub-national groups. Any attempt to move beyond this 'struggle in the struggle' involves separating out women's gender struggles from other sites of difference and conflict, such as race, class, sexuality and generation.[9] This implies that gender transformation through revolutionary struggle requires a type of consciousness that can move beyond the mobilisation of gender stereotypes to define appropriate participation and representation of women's experiences of struggle. Pettman outlines the development of such a consciousness as 'a move from female consciousness, which seeks rights or safety within family and gender expectations within the nationalist struggle, to feminist consciousness, where activist women view women's liberation as an intrinsic part of national liberation and seek social transformation' (1996: 125).

Without such a shift in gender transformations, Enloe (2002; 1988) argues, the militarised masculinity that relies on women's exclusion or 'otherness' carries its momentum into post-war public life. The drive for stability, normality and public order influences the post-war phase of statebuilding and reconstruction. The re-emergence of family and community are central to this vision of 'return to normality' and women are repositioned in the domestic sphere to ensure stability. The public/private division is reinforced and any socio-political empowerment or changes in gender relations emerging from the war are dissolved.

Often, the increased militarisation of the state as it absorbs the male fighters and the political leaders serves to further marginalise and threaten women in the post-war setting. In this script even the women who crossed the gender divide to fight and carry arms struggle to hold on to their status as liberation army veterans. While such analysis focuses largely on earlier anti-colonial wars such as Zimbabwe, Nicaragua and Mozambique, the dynamics of unfulfilled expectations of transformation and the reinforcement of gendered assumptions about women's roles and position they reveal can be found in contemporary post-conflict development programmes. The same arguments apply in terms of calls for stability and a return or restoration of the state and society. Women are marginalised in the peacebuilding and statebuilding processes that are very often tied to peace agreements brokered with militias, warlords and others who must be appeased and given power and roles in the new order. This has been observed in the weakness of the disarmament, demobilisation and reintegration (DDR) programmes for women ex-combatants in Liberia, many of them child soldiers at the height of the war and abandoned as misfitting women in the post-war peace (Specht 2006; Amnesty International 2008).

Overall, the focus on gender roles, while illuminating, does not necessarily reflect the spectrum of roles and the inherent contradictions among them that typify survival in war-affected areas. Women can be at once mothers, rebels, farmers, prostitutes, refugees, aid recipients, wives, sell-outs, and community leaders. Men too can be leaders, humiliated bystanders, protectors, perpetrators of violence, warlords, soldiers, rebels, fathers, sons and husbands. Capturing these dynamics and understanding difference is another theme found in the writings on women and war. Feminist criticism in both Gender and Development and International Relations has grappled with, and been enriched by, arguments of 'difference'; that women are not homogeneous groups and do not constitute a fixed 'subject' of enquiry or action in pursuit of liberation, equality or resistance (Sylvester 1994; Pettman 1996; Jabri and O' Gorman 1999). In many contexts women and gender interact with other workings of power such as nationality, ethnicity, sexuality, age, poverty and class in the construction and living of identities as women in particular places. Chandra Mohanty (1988; 1995) challenges Western feminism as a 'discursive colonialism' that creates a homogeneous 'other' in 'Third World Woman' who must be problematised and explained by a white Western 'self'. In understanding women from the non-Western world, she argues, '[w]hat matters is the complex, historical range of power differences, commonalities and resistances that exist among women in Africa which construct African women as 'subjects' of their own politics' (1988: 84).

To understand gender and power in practice within conflict and post-conflict environments remains very necessary: despite some notable developments, gender still largely translates as women. This is true in both academic and policy work on gender, violence, security and peace. Some ground-breaking work has been done in exploring masculinities and male roles in relation to violence and militarism; much of this has built on the foundational work of Rob (Raewyn) Connell (2000; 2002) who writes of multiple masculinities and the role of social construction in creating these and in shaping a hegemonic male gendered identity in different settings – war, sport, business – where certain roles or stereotypes may be hegemonic but are not necessarily commonly shared or easily experienced by all men or even most men.[10] The gendered stereotypes are found in the shaping of security sector reform and disarmament programmes that often exclude women combatants or treat them in a tokenistic manner while making general assumptions of power and hypermasculinity for male soldiers and combatants. They also define the recent growing interest in programmes targeting youth, radicalisation, gangs and urban violence in countries where a demographic youth bulge fuels fears and stereotypes of feral male youth as needing to be contained. The work of Henri Myrttinen (2003; 2008) on disarmament and masculinity and on violence and power in Timor-Leste highlights the prescribed role for men in war and violence; he shows how these constrain and also fail to grasp how dynamic the identities of masculinity are. Current work on male identities in conflict and violence is also emerging from the necessity and challenges of developing aid programmes aimed at ex-combatants and dealing with the legacies of war, gender and violence that often persist into peace, recovery and development. These arguments are self-evident if we consider that the critical engagement of women's prescribed roles and hegemonic femininity has been the sword of feminist analysis. One collection (Bannon and Correia 2006) explores very pressing themes – including young men and gender in war and post-war reconstruction; and male youth, conflict, and urbanization – looking at cases such as Sierra Leone and Rwanda.

Women, peace and security: an international policy framework

UN Security Council Resolution 1325, as text and practice, has already been the subject of feminist academic analysis; in the field, it has been debated as a triumph of advocacy by civil society activists and women's organisations working at a global level, and by 'femocrats' within international organisations (Shepherd 2008; Cohn et al. 2004). The verdict, however, will rest on the ongoing implementation of that resolution. Examples of gender and development analysis encountering war and conflict include the work of Oxfam during the 1990s and the Institute of Development Studies (IDS) at the University of Sussex, notably

2000–2010: A decade of women, peace and security at the UN

SCR 1325 (2000)

In October 2010 the United Nations gathered to 'celebrate' the tenth anniversary of a landmark Security Council decision: Resolution 1325 (2000) on women, peace and security.[11] This resolution finally acknowledged the impact of war on women across the world and set out the political imperative to protect women from targeted acts of violence and to ensure the greater participation of women in all aspects of peacemaking, peacekeeping and peacebuilding. The global agenda for international peace and security had at last accepted the importance of gender in understanding violence and transforming the prospects for peace and security, or so it seemed.

UNSCR 1325, adopted on 31 October 2000, called on member states to:
- reaffirm existing commitments under humanitarian law as applied to women;
- reaffirm specific undertakings such as the Beijing Platform of Action;
- consider different needs of male and female ex-combatants;
- end impunity and seek to prosecute those responsible for war crimes, including rape and sexual violence;
- mainstream a gender perspective into peace operations;
- take into account gender considerations and the rights of women in UN missions; and
- increase participation of women in decision making and peace-making at all levels.

In follow-up more detailed reports were commissioned on the state of women, peace and security to inform how 1325 would be taken forward. UNIFEM commissioned an independent report in 2002, 'Women, War, and Peace', conducted by Elisabeth Rehn, (the former Finnish Defence Minister and UN Special Rapporteur on Human Rights in Bosnia-Herzegovina), and Ellen Johnson Sirleaf (now the first woman President of Liberia and coming to the end of a first elected term). The UNIFEM study was hard-hitting and brought to notice from the ground up the very real challenges that were affecting women in war-torn countries: the targeted violence, the lack of focus in recon-struction programmes, and the virtual absence of women from the negotiation tables of peace processes around the world. These findings were further affirmed in another 2002 study on 'Women, Peace and Security' prepared in follow up to UNSCR 1325 and submitted to the Security Council.

SCR 1820 (2008)

The framework of commitments in SCR 1325 was reinforced in 2008 by the adoption of SCR 1820, which focused on specific actions to combat sexual violence in conflict, including better prevention and protection strategies during war as well as measures to end the impunity of per-petrators. SCR 1820 was driven by the brutal facts on the ground during a decade of war and violence in the eastern Democratic Republic of Congo, compounding generations of such atrocities of rape in war that in some measure had been acknowledged by the International Criminal Tribunals for Rwanda and the former Yugoslavia.

In February 2010 a dedicated Special Representative for Sexual Violence in Conflict was appointed by the Secretary-General in accor-dance with SCR 1888 of September 2009, a sequel to SCR 1820. The network UN Action against Sexual Violence in Conflict (UN Action) has 13 UN entities as members and supports the implementation of SCR 1820, providing a ready platform for the new SRSG.

SCR 1820, particularly, has rested on the need for sound data to 'make the case' for sexual violence in conflict as a security issue, and rape as a war crime. There is a working assumption in the interna-tional debates at present that the issue needs to meet a 'threshold of credibility',[12] and paragraph 15 of the resolution explicitly requests improvement to data collection and analysis to inform implementation of the resolution.

Sources: UN Security Council (2000); UN Security Council (2008a); Rehn and Johnson Sirleaf (2002); UN (2002); UN (2010b)

through its BRIDGE project and reports. Specialist NGOS and think tanks such as ACORD and International Alert have also been at the forefront of investigation and analysis of gender, conflict and development.[13] These are all efforts to examine the tensions between gender equality, conflict resolution and peace-building in development policies and programmes.

Two distinctive approaches can be identified in terms of the implementation of SCR 1325. The first is integrating the resolution into existing policy frameworks. An example of this is the inclusion of a chapter on gender in the Security Sector Reform handbook issued by the OECD Development Assistance Committee (OECD DAC 2009).[14] The second approach has been to develop dedicated policy frameworks and action plans. The ICRC, the UN (including UNIFEM), specialist NGOs like International Alert, and the European Commission and EU member states have all commissioned background work to inform political decision making and aid strategies in response to a growing momentum around women, peace and security. Sixteen National Action Plans now exist globally for the implementation of SCR 1325. This does not include the EU Comprehensive Approach, adopted in December 2008. Only three of these plans, however, are from conflict-affected countries (Côte d'Ivoire, Liberia and Uganda) where action on women, peace and security should be a priority. Twelve of the plans relate to Western donor governments. As noted in the box above, the UN also appointed a Special Representative on Sexual Violence in 2009 with a dedicated remit to ensure that actions to end sexual violence in conflict become an integral part of UN operations.

A shared challenge of both the 'mainstreaming' and 'stand-alone' approaches is ensuring that interventions are responding to particular situations rather than pre-existing programmes, mandates or institutional structures. SCR 1325 and its successor resolutions (SCRs 1820, 1888 and 1889) have also generated a raft of new programming on women, peace and security by inter-national agencies and NGOs. Examples include: UNIFEM support to women's participation in peacemaking and formal peace processes, including in Darfur; International Refugee Council projects on sexual and gender-based violence in Liberia and the DRC, offering medical services, psycho-social counselling and support for community reintegration and livelihoods to women who have been subject to sexual violence; and the Women in Peacebuilding Programme (WIPNET) in West Africa, active in the Liberian peace process and continuing to build a constituency for women's participation in peacemaking at local, national and regional levels.

Peacekeeping operations have long been a male and military bastion of the UN. However, gender advisers are now more prominent in UN peace operations: by 2005, ten of the eighteen peace operations at that time had advisers, including the DRC, Afghanistan, Liberia, Timor-Leste and Sudan (UN DPKO 2005). Currently, some 30 per cent of civilian personnel serving across the 16 UN peace operations are women. Only 7 per cent of the civilian police component (of 13,000) and 2 per cent of the military contingent (of 87,000) are women, yet this is progress.[15] That the UN's Department of Peacekeeping Operations (DPKO) has produced gender statistics mission by mission on a monthly basis since mid-2006 is testimony to the impact of SCR 1325 on perceptions of mission.[16] Part of this push for gender advisers in peacekeeping did come from that landmark resolution. But a resistant culture of militaristic and operational masculinity often defines peacekeeping and humanitarian operations in particular. As if to drive this point home, media and political reactions to cases of sexual exploitation and abuse of authority (SEA) by military and civilian UN personnel – notably in peace operations in West Africa and the DRC – was as much a driver as SCR 1325 for gender approaches coming onto the operational agenda.

Gender assumptions and DDR programming in Liberia

Other gender aspects of the reality of war need fuller recognition. For example, young boys aged 10–18 form a very vulnerable group, often being the target of militias and rebels as the so-called child soldiers who are the fodder of many wars. The impact of this is ongoing in disarmament, demobilisation, and reintegration (DDR) programmes when the children return as men; leaving camp life and reintegration into family and community is often a painful process, and a rise in domestic violence often accompanies the peace dividend of demobilised militants. The taking of weapons and payment of an allowance is as far as 'DD' often goes, and 'R' might mean some short-term training and a reintegration allowance of a small lump sum. However, the architects of these programmes rarely look to the mother, sister, wife, and children waiting for this man they have not seen for years; everyone has changed, and so the challenge of household reintegration is often painful and long-term.

Studies of girls' experiences of DDR in Liberia demonstrate how gender questioning can open up very practical insights into why such processes fail girls and women, or fail to take account of gendered realities of risk and post-conflict challenges for fighters, wives and supporters returning from the rebel camps. Specht (2006) identifies factors such as the exclusion of girl soldiers/camp supporters from the lists compiled by commanders for DDR registration; the confiscation of arms by the commanders, leaving the girls without a gun to trade for money and access to the programme; the giving of cash transfers to girls that create new risks and vulnerabilities with boyfriends and families; and the delay in the launch of the process, so that girls have been forced into taking up risky livelihood alternatives such as prostitution, migration, street trading or entering into abusive relationships. Some girls were already teen mothers and so could not leave their children to enter the camps; others have suffered in the rebel camps and did not want to re-enter any form of camp life.

Well-documented trends, include the rise in local prostitution as in all militarised situations, has been a part of UN peacekeeping since it began. Vulnerable girls and women who need access to food, cash and resources see the income-generating possibilities. More specifically, there has been growing awareness and reporting of direct abuse and violence by peacekeepers and civilian staff towards women who are in their protection. This has resulted in international standards in the form of codes of conduct and accountability mechanisms within and among humanitarian organisations to enforce such standards.[17] As a result, applying SCR 1325 and its successor resolutions has meant challenging some uncomfortable facts and dilemmas about the role of protectors and providers of aid themselves in contributing to risk and insecurity for women affected by war. Policies and action plans will not change the realities on the ground overnight, but it is a clear indication that the message has been received and understood at the highest political level that women and children will be protected even from the protector.

Contemporary wars and international interventions

Our understanding of and responses to the issue of women, peace and security remain tested and urgent in contemporary wars that continue their ranging, violent and chronic dynamics. The accelerated government military offensive from January until May 2009 in the north of Sri Lanka corralled civilians alongside the LTTE guerrillas (Liberation Tigers of Tamil Eelam, known more colloquially as the Tamil Tigers) as they were driven into smaller and smaller pockets of territory. By April 2009 some 80,000–120,000 thousand trapped individuals (civilians and insurgents) shared a strip of land which offered little in the way of either shelter or escape. The government treated the trapped civilians as combatants who chose to remain, and the LTTE treated them as human shields and hostages to make the last stand.

In the Democratic Republic of Congo conflict, which has been described as Africa's World War, the issue of rape as a weapon of war, and the prevalence of sexual violence in the eastern part of the country, have provided the impetus for international action. With a potpourri of militias as well as the official armed forces and UN peacekeepers on the ground, the militarised and insecure context persists. Indeed the government armed forces (FARDC) themselves are a mixed outcome of recurrent efforts to integrate various militias, further destabilising a relatively undisciplined and unaccountable security sector. This has placed the UN mission there in the difficult position of pursuing both a mandate to enforce disarmament of militias in the eastern DRC whilst also providing protection for civilians. A report to the UN Security Council in 2008 highlights this commitment gap, stating that there are an estimated 10 peacekeepers for every 10,000 civilians in North Kivu alone; this underscores the magnitude of aspiration for prevention and protection with regard to sexual violence in the eastern part of the country (UN Security Council 2008b). In July/August 2010 there was another round of mass atrocities in the form of systematic rape cases in the region of Walikale, North Kivu in the eastern DRC. The report to the UN Security Council on the implementation of SCR 1820 in December 2010 found that:

> Sexual violence has also served to clear communities out of min-ing areas that in turn fund and prolong conflict. The mass rapes in Walikale, DRC, indicate a connection between the illicit exploitation of natural resources, continuing operations of illegal armed groups, and high levels of violence against women. This series of mass rapes occurred in conjunction with looting and pillage by the Democratic Forces for the Liberation of Rwanda

(FDLR) and Mayi-Mayi Cheka, whose members rounded up women and prevented them from fleeing the besieged villages. Three hundred and three cases were reported, with many women having been gang-raped by up to five or six men at a time. (UN 2010b, para. 11)

In Iraq, Nadje Al-Ali and Nicola Pratt (2009) reveal the negative impact of the international intervention and give depth to the complexity and agency of women's lives under the occupation. They explore why the international intervention has not only failed to liberate women but also used the political capital of women's rights to justify wider statebuilding and stabilisation agendas and concerns that, in part, undermine and worsen the situation and position of women in Iraq. Frequent lip service is paid to SCR 1325 by the international community in Baghdad, but in implementation it fails to account for the violence against women from many sources in Iraq, as well as their absence from decision making on peace and development programmes. Al-Ali and Pratt focus on women who have been widowed, displaced and impoverished into dangerous livelihoods to show up the workings and the failures of security, protection and humanitarian aid to help them. They show how women are constituted as subjects of politics by many actors with little reference to women's own opinions or experiences; women become a battleground for ideologies on all sides as to who is an Iraqi woman, who protects her, and how she should conduct herself. The focus on systemic and structural dynamics and relationships brings feminist analysis, and analysis of war more generally, back again to its core and away from the depoliticised and sanitised roles that persist and shape many policies, programmes and studies of women in war: namely, women as victims, as aberrant females, as mothers; or elite women as token figures of congratulation.

Afghanistan and Iraq present very new and different wars in terms of the global context of the 'war on terror' and the merging of military and aid interventions in new and ambiguous ways that challenge and distort the lines of peacekeeping, counter-insurgency, humanitarian assistance, and peacebuilding. Yet on closer examination, while these countries present unique and differing perspectives of modern warfare, there is much that reflects the universal continuities of people caught up in violent conflict as embattled communities dealing with all-comers. Lina Abirafeh (2009) provides a unique perspective, having worked with the 'aid apparatus' in Afghanistan and also conducted in-depth interviews and research with women and men from Afghan communities at different levels. She gives voice to the backlash that women have suffered from the approach of the international intervention to gender programming, while demonstrating how the technocratic approach of gender as part of the military and aid objectives in counterinsurgency and peacebuilding creates its own inherent contradictions and failures. The failures are many: lack of understanding of the importance of religion and Islamic culture in the lives of women in Afghanistan; missing the significance of the country's historical experience of resisting foreign interventions; the urban and elite bias that motivates engagement with and resources for women, yet denies their own agency, coping mechanisms and resources. In holding up this mirror, Abirafeh also reveals the hope of rescuing 'gender and conflict' from itself.

Contemporary wars in very different places are producing common insights and echoing historical lessons on women and war: that policy makers and aid workers are repeating assumptions and failing to learn from the past in shaping the assistance and protection provided in international operations; that women's lives and identities and how they are constructed as subjects of war by various parties (including those called on as peacekeepers and protectors) mean in practice that they often become the battleground for other wars of states, religions, and resources. As Enloe cautions, 'when on occasion women's liberation is wielded instrumentally by any masculinised elite as a rationale-of-convenience for their actions, we should be on high alert; they'll put it back on the shelf just as soon as it no longer serves their longer-range purpose' (Cohn and Enloe 2003: 1203).

Conclusion

We are reminded that violent conflict operates at many levels and that development and political solutions bring their own risks and assumptions, placing women and men in certain roles and identities and ensuring that war, militarism and privileged types of warring masculinities and victimised femininities on all sides perpetuate violence. In the lineage of feminist criticism such insights hold relevance also in the Democratic Republic of Congo, where women as victims of rape and sexual violence threatens to become the only story of women and war that will endure. Understanding how women are at risk and how they survive is critical to building on women's agency and dignity as mothers, girls, women, wives, daughters, refugees, community activists and leaders, educators, farmers and businesswomen. It is this focus on agency that ultimately must drive the goals of recovery and peacebuilding. The challenge ahead is ensuring that UN SCR 1325 remains a political agenda and not allowing it to become a technocratic one. This means looking at outcomes in terms of transformation of the roles, institutional contexts and everyday lives of women – amidst insecurity, poverty and violence – and not just at outputs in terms of projects by driven by results-based management. In a wider sense feminist analysis, or more correctly what Cynthia Enloe calls 'feminist curiosity', holds great promise and the prospect of using the current focus on complex peacebuilding and statebuilding operations to drive a rigorous and radical critique of the overall conflict and development architecture. Feminist critique has long experience of challenging the structural workings of power and institutions that render the international personal. The recent openings in terms of engaging differentiated masculinities in war and peace, as well as the investigation of the realities of the 'war on terror', 'security' and 'stabilisation' for women in Iraq and Afghanistan, are evidence of that prospect.

6 | Fragile States and the Limits of Peacebuilding and Statebuilding

This book ends by assessing the current dominance of the peace-building/statebuilding axis. To what extent does it indicate the overreach of development policies and programmes in conflict zones? As seen throughout this book, the agenda of conflict and development has brought forth new dilemmas: how can soldiers, diplomats and aid workers work together in conflict situations? How do we classify development assistance in complex situations and not squeeze traditional poverty reduction programmes? Is aid always compromised in war-affected situations? How do we measure success? While more explicitly development-centred approaches to human security informed the early shaping of security and development programmes, there are concerns that the policy shift to fragile states in response to the reconceptualisation of threats may have changed the paradigm. Even in the face of the global and interconnected nature of insecurity across a range of issues, the notion of human security itself is under pressure as military and state-centric security re-emerges as the dominant interest.

The main criticisms made of contemporary peace operations in conflict-affected countries are the nature of their universal claims as defenders of peace and democracy, the top-down imposition of common approaches to programmes in different settings, a state-centric bias, the promotion of institutional rationality, and a dismissive approach to local realities. These critiques of the 'liberal peace' and the disparaging use of the term that now requires quotation marks, also make certain assumptions about the concepts, actors, approaches and outcomes of the international peace, security and development architecture.

Current dilemmas of development and conflict

Securing whom from what?
The securitisation of aid is a major theme of the relationship between conflict and development and reflects the recurring tensions between human and military security outlined in Chapter 4. The concern with fragile states can be viewed in Duffield's words as the 'reproblematisation of security in terms of underdevelopment becoming dangerous' such that that the role of development in peacebuilding and conflict prevention is recast within '[a] new security framework … in which stability is now regarded as unfeasible without development, while development is non-sustainable without stability' (2001: 259). It is clear that the 'war on terror' has transformed understandings of security. Within the definition of human development, a focus on human security for poor people in the context of poverty has shifted to a concern with the threat the poor pose to global security. As Beall et al. point out, frequently in discussions of the security–development nexus 'it is unclear whose security is being referred to; a sharp distinction needs to be drawn between the security of those people in the countries where development is being pursued and security in the country of the donor' (2006: 60). The risks of merging counter-terror and development programmes is not simply the crowding out of poverty reduction as the basis for development, but the risk of contributing to the failure of development in all its dimensions and security in all its dimensions. The shift to a narrower counter-terrorism notion of security also generates a paradox whereby the central emphasis given to state–society relations and

negotiations in peacebuilding/statebuilding is directly challenged by the cover governments have received to undermine and label civil society groups and dissidents (Howell 2006).

Local engagement and ownership

> Put simply, people must own their own peace: it has to begin, grow and become embedded in people's minds. It follows that peacebuilding can only happen within communities and within a country.... [I]t must go beyond mantra to substance. (UN 2010a: paras 17 and 19)

Reflecting a core critique of the neo-liberal interpretation of state-building and peacebuilding, Richmond (2008a: 113) sees such approaches as 'romanticising the local' in four particular ways to justify the top-down imposition of programmes and approaches: local people are viewed as exotic and unknown; as lacking capacity; as devious and not to be trusted; or as resources to be co-opted into projects. Critics themselves, however, are equally guilty of valorising the local without taking sufficient account of the range of actors for war and peace that constitute the local reality: peaceful NGOs cannot be the only actors for peace if sustained peace is to be achieved. Much of the commentary on local engagement treats the 'local' as monolithic, passive and imposed upon with no agency, resistance or negotiation on the parts of local elites, people and communities – and certainly no complicity in violence or threats to peace. The result is a uniform lack of any specific understanding of who exactly is local.

Béatrice Pouligny (2006) counters this with an analytic perspective titled *Peace Operations Seen from Below*, and gives substance to the ubiquitous calls for local ownership. In so doing, she problematises the 'local' as a varied and insecure space of many agents and drills down to the interactive dynamics of UN–local relations in different locations including El Salvador,

Cambodia and Haiti. She charts the way in which the new multi-dimensional peace operations may seem superficial, removed from people's lives, and yet simultaneously penetrate the fabric of the country and society in unprecedented ways: 'one may predict that [the interventions] potentially affect large components of these societies, precisely at a time when crucial elements of the relations between political and social order are renegotiated' (2006: x).

In this context, the UN interactions with local peoples are understood as 'plural and dynamic' rather than passive, and can also be both negative and positive. The actors who constitute the local space are many and cannot be reduced, she argues, to the simple separation of 'civil society versus failed state' – and individual actors, indeed, may take on a mix of sometimes contradictory roles to manage the fluid power relations in their environment in order to survive its instability (Pouligny 2006: 42–4). For example a local human rights activist being funded by a Western agency may also be a village elder, locally elected councillor and relative of the local warlord. The 'intermingling of allegiances and loyalties is often difficult to grasp' (2006: 56). The UN and other outside actors often do not fully understand or appreciate this fluidity, and need to give more attention to context analysis and the networks that mediate local relationships. As international actors become involved they are already part of these intermingling networks and are not always aware of the ways in which this positioning operates or is perceived. Decisions about who to partner with and fund may unjustly privilege certain well-placed local actors. The dance of partners includes an emergent and often weak government, also seeking out and cautious about local actors, and different community and development groups. Civil society is also often implicated in the conflict and its legacies – rather than necessarily being an alternative to a perceived failing state. Understanding the change dynamics of international engagement in this complex local context is therefore critical to success.

These debates on the nature of the 'local' and how to engage have a flip side in posing another dilemma: the role of experts on peace and development. Uma Kothari (2005b) provides a very powerful critique of the development 'industry' and the role of 'expertise' and 'experts' in reinforcing power relations of donor and recipient as 'self' and 'other'. In this she finds local articulation and forms of dissent are appropriated or rendered technocratic, and so robbed of their agency and autonomy. This power of the neo-liberal enterprise leads Kothari and others to see international development (most obviously in conflict-affected countries) as an extension or reassertion of Western colonial authority – a view that it is difficult, on the face of it, to dispute. Yet it is a very simplistic understanding of power as asymmetrical and top-down, and always a case of winner and losers. Similarly Oliver Richmond sees the peacebuilding approaches advanced in the new generation of peace operations as

> 'normalising' governance activities involving the transfer of liberal epistemology into conflict zones. This offers an ontology in which peace is plausible and positive within a framework of liberal governance, regulation and freedom, and a methodology in which its construction is simply a rational and technical problem-solving matter. (2008a: 116)

Yet these analyses assume capacities, coherence and coordination that is fictional; they do not reflect the inevitable and necessary tensions within international development interventions in conflict zones (not least the range of actors and agendas), what constitutes 'local ownership', and the lack of consensus about exit points for international interventions.

State collapse and alternative governance

> Collapse means that the basic functions of the state are no longer performed.... As the decision-making centre of government, the

state is paralysed and inoperative: laws are not made, order is not preserved, and societal cohesion is not enhanced…. As a symbol of identity, it has lost its power of conferring a name on its - people and a meaning to their social action…. As a territory, it is no longer assured security and provisioning by a central sovereign organisation…. As the authoritative political institution, it has lost legitimacy, which is therefore up for grabs, and so has lost its right to command and conduct public affairs…. As a system of socio-economic organization, its functional balance of inputs and outputs is destroyed; it no longer receives support from nor exercises controls over its people, and it no longer is even the target of demands, because its people know that it is incapable of providing supplies. No longer functioning, with neither traditional nor charismatic nor institutional sources of legitimacy, it has lost the right to rule. (Zartman 1995: 5)

In media and political coverage, peacebuilding and statebuilding have been referred to interchangeably or conflated with 'nation building' which is something quite distinct to statebuilding. As discussed in Chapter 2 with regard to nationalism and identities, the idea of nation refers to the generation of collective identity by people through culture, symbols and traditions that may or may not necessarily be tied to territory. The Western nation-state, where people and territory are coterminous, is a relatively recent phenomenon following long decades, even centuries of evolution (Tilly 1975). This idea of nation and the quite distinct idea of state (which focuses in essence on the development of organisation and structures of national and local government) have come to be conflated and confused in describing governance and development approaches in conflict zones. The terms nation building and statebuilding go beyond technocratic prescriptions of rule of law, constitution building, and delivery of public services to signify the loaded political debates of global, unilateral Western intervention and regime change in

Afghanistan and Iraq, neo-colonial governance in the experiences of transitional administration in Kosovo and Timor-Leste, and neo-liberal designs of the nature of peace in all these cases and extending to the DRC and Sudan. Yet at its heart statebuilding remains a concern about functioning states in an international order that can protect and provide for their people and ensure internal and external security. Nation building without the grandiosity is revealed to be the social contract of state and society in terms of legitimacy and accountability. It is also about the basic delivery of services to citizens to enable a functioning society and economy.

The 'transitional administration' mandates of the UN in Timor-Leste and Kosovo are examples where the UN, on behalf of the international community, has governed in a trusteeship manner. This has brought with it shades of the arrogance of power, on the one hand, and, on the other, the 'destined to fail' impossible aims of sweeping mandates and expectations to build a state within 6–12 month mandate extensions and arduously negotiated and inevitably insufficient budgets. On 27 September 2002 Timor-Leste became the 191st member of the United Nations and the world's newest independent state, having declared independence on 20 May 2002 following a referendum in 1999 and an interim UN administration during 1999–2002 (UNTAET).

The mandate of this mission was overarching: UN Security Council Resolution 1272 (1999) made the UN the *de facto* government of the country to prepare for independence. The mission, under the leadership of the Secretary-General's Special Representative Sergio Vieira de Mello, was 'endowed with overall responsibility for the administration of East Timor and … empowered to exercise all legislative and executive authority, including the administration of justice'. While considered successful in terms of the declaration of independence for East Timor in

Independence in Timor-Leste

Independence marked the end of a long and brutal history of colonialism, occupation and resistance. Colonised by Portugal, and occupied by Indonesia (1975–99), a post-independent Timor-Leste state faces significant challenges in forging a national identity, constructing national dialogue, building the capacities of government across the board, and ending the poverty and marginalisation of its people. With a population of just over one million people, defined by a fast-growing young population and high fertility rate (7.8), Timor–Leste holds many possibilities and risks that are intertwined in its push to build its state, economy and society. Notwithstanding regional factors such as the dominance of Australia and relations with Indonesia, as well as national income from oil resources off the coast, the conflict risks and challenges faced by Timor-Leste have a strong internal dimension.

The independence of Timor-Leste has been defined by the shifting mandates of five UN missions. The United Nations Mission in East Timor (UNAMET) (June–October 1999) was a political mission mandated to organise and conduct a popular consultation to ascertain the future status of East Timor. The United Nations Transitional Administration in East Timor (UNTAET) (October 1999–May 2002) was a peacekeeping operation established by the Security Council following rejection by the East Timorese of special autonomy. It exercised administrative authority over East Timor during the transition to independence. The United Nations Mission of Support in East Timor (UNMISET) (May 2002—May 2005), also a peacekeeping mission, was mandated to provide assistance to the newly independent Timor-Leste until all operational responsibilities were fully devolved to the national authorities.

Once the peacekeeping mission withdrew, a new political mission, the United Nations Office in Timor-Leste (UNOTIL) (May 2005–August 2006), supported the development of critical state institutions and the police, and provided training in observance of democratic governance and human rights. The UN returned in force following the 2006 crisis, in the form of the ongoing United Nations Integrated Mission in Timor-Leste (UNMIT). It has an extensive mandate covering policing, capacity building for policing, security sector review, national dialogue, and working with government through the UN agencies, funds and pro-grammes (UN Country Team) on implementing national development plans. This mandate is expected to be reconsidered, with possible draw-down of the mission, following the 2012 elections. There is pressure for UNMIT to support the government in establishing key foundations in terms of security and national dialogue before the inevitable draw-down of the mission.

2002, the mission has been subject to hard-hitting criticisms. One major critique is the lack of local contacts and engagement by the mission, and the failure to deliver dividends of reconstruction and services sufficient to secure the new country against state failure (Chopra 2002). Another assessment suggests that the mission was simply not equipped to fulfil its governing and statebuilding mandate and was geared for peacekeeping rather than nation building (Suhrke 2001). Paris (2004: 220) has a more construc-tive view of UNTAET's mission, seeing it as a demonstration of the usually lacking international commitment to the long haul. He describes the transitional administration as a 'model of asser-tive peacebuilding' owing to the 'willingness of peacebuilders to assume full responsibility for the reconstruction of a functioning state apparatus'.

However, the nature of the state that emerged from inter-national support (not just the UN, but leading donors including Australia, Portugal, Japan and, increasingly, China) needs reflec-tion, too. The adage of 'humpty dumpty' is apt: all these king's horses and all these king's men have not been able to put it together again. Statebuilding in Timor-Leste has been fraught with the tensions and paradoxes of its colonial legacy and current experience of international involvement. A thorny issue is the heavy reliance upon, and high aid costs of, a rapidly revolving cadre of international advisers in government ministries: concerns about high salaries and the qualifications and experience of many personnel have been expressed. The adoption of Portuguese as an official language of the country and the use of English as the *lingua franca* of the international presence, in a context where most of the population do not speak either language, have deep implications for capacity-building efforts and also affect directly the ability of people to claim rights and services – most notably in access to education and justice. Tetun (an official language) and Bahasa (Indonesian) are widely spoken in the country.

International interest in Timor-Leste gained new momentum in the aftermath of a crisis in 2006 prompted by splits within the army, and between the army and police, that spilled over into clashes on the streets and resulted in some 42 people being killed, at least 40 being injured, and over 70,000 people displaced.[1] The violence triggered a wave of attacks across the country, including beatings and house burnings as many grievances erupted, unchecked. A review of donor practices in the light of the 2006 crisis, commissioned by the Norwegian aid agency NORAD, highlights the extent to which development actors had neglected the risk of conflict or violence in the design of their programmes in the 2002–6 period. The review assesses how far aid policies and spending compounded imbalances that contributed to conflict tensions – finding an overemphasis on statebuilding in the capital and central government, insufficient attention to micro-economic and employment efforts, and a lack of focus on the emergence of political and economic exclusion across the country (Norad 2007).

Fresh presidential and parliamentary elections in 2007 were marked by controversy as FRETELIN, the party that grew from the Timorese resistance to Indonesian occupation, was voted out of power and initially resisted accepting the outcome. A further flashpoint was provided by attacks on the President and Prime Minister in February 2008 by renegade army officers. However, these flashpoints in themselves are seen as symptoms of more systemic and historical tensions and unresolved conflicts in Timor-Leste; they threaten to become cleavages for future, more violent conflict if they are not fully addressed. There is a consensus among local and international actors that these issues include: the proper functioning of police and army in a democratic state; a process of national dialogue along with a strengthened and functioning justice system to heal the past and build foundations for a shared future; building the capacities and functions of state, economy and society; and delivering tangible evidence of peace and development to the people of Timor-Leste, almost ten years after independence.

The limitations of international support to Timor-Leste do not remove the need and responsibility for political leaders to lead the building of appropriate state institutions accountable to all citizens. In this they collectively face the challenges of overcoming urban–rural, generational and gender tensions and disparities, and addressing the enduring legacies of the long war of independence: human rights atrocities and delayed justice; revolutionary faction fighting; and unfinished demobilisation and reintegration. Timor-Leste reflects the necessary international, national and local interactions and tensions that define post-conflict development and peacebuilding.

State fragility may entail assistance and international interventions, as part of search for legitimacy and resilience, that have the counter-productive potential to destabilise and be in themselves a cause of external shocks: the infamous World Bank economic structural adjustment programmes of the 1980s are a salutary example. Paris (2004) advocates 'institutionalisation before liberalisation' as a remedy to the quick fixes and rushed benchmarks (such as elections) of the first wave of new UN peace operations that faltered or relapsed into conflict. In his analysis, peacebuilding and statebuilding are not events but processes of preparing for peace and development on a sound basis of endogenous institutions, both to assure governance and to 'minimise the detabililising effects of the liberalisation process' in fragile post-conflict settings.

Current configurations of statebuilding and peacebuilding can also learn from the debate in development circles about 'good enough' governance as a counter to the long list of policy agendas and perfect models. Grindle (2004: 535) suggests that a 'good enough' governance agenda would be based on 'a more nuanced understanding of the evolution of institutions and government capabilities; being explicit about trade-offs and priorities in a world in which all good things cannot be pursued at once; learning about what's working rather than focusing solely on governance gaps; taking the role of government in poverty alleviation seriously, and grounding action in the contextual realities of each country'.

Rethinking state failure in Somalia

Somalia presents a conundrum to the international community: the ultimate failed state is also testimony to the nature of resilience *without* a state, and thus dislodges a basic assumption of the conflict and development agenda – that underdevelopment begets war begets underdevelopment in self-perpetuating crisis (Bradbury 2008; Berdal 2005; Menkhaus 2004). The sources cited stress that they are not underplaying the nature and extent of violence and instability in Somalia, but emphasise that international aid and military intervention have largely failed – and failed to take account of what makes Somalia resilient.

Mark Bradbury examines how Somaliland, in the north-west of the former Somalia, defies the premises of peace building as 'a self-governing territory' that is not a state but demonstrates aspects of statehood – including an elected government, collection of taxes, management of services and borders, intervention in the market and provision of security for citizens. Somaliland reveals through cattle exports, banking and trading how a vibrant economy operates without the formal workings of a state and is inserted into the globalised political economy in various ways. Bradbury argues that '[o]ne of the paradoxes of international engagement in Somalia is that while diplomacy and statebuilding have focused on re-establishing a sovereign government Somalis themselves have fashioned varied forms of governance within the territory of the former Republic' (2008: 245). He cites other factors for the emergence of Somaliland as 'a stable polity' that include an active civil society, reliance on customary law and the traditional leadership of the pastoralist economy and society. He terms this phenomenon 'pastoral democracy' in a fusion of traditional and modern governance practices to restore order, provide security to citizens, mediate power relations and establish property rights and ownership.

Matt Berdal (2005: 697) highlights the 'the self-generated demobilisation process' that defies international DDR and SSR approaches: 'Developments in local governance over the past decade or so also help to explain the striking success of the disarmament and demobilisation of ex-combatants in Somalia since 1994; striking because it has occurred in the absence of central government, unaccompanied by security-sector reform and national reconciliation, and without any assistance from external actors.'The case of Somalia invites the international community to look not only to the collapse of government or the failures of development for the chronic situation, but also to the failure of aid and military interventions, and to look more closely at what survives and how it survives.

Mark Bradbury, in writing about Somaliland (2008), calls for 'greater diplomatic creativity' and 'international acceptance of alternative formulations of state governance'. Such alternatives are also considered by Alex de Waal (2009) in his counter argument to liberal institutions as he considers contexts where 'social affinities and patronage networks' may hold greater sway and where the 'patrimonial marketplace' is the organising mechanism as influence is negotiated and traded in various ways with internal and external actors. These analyses of alternatives apply more widely and need to be engaged more seriously by the international architecture of missions, resources and efforts.

The Afghanisation of development as peacebuilding
The exceptional cases of Iraq and Afghanistan are both driving changes in the understanding and practice of peacebuilding and statebuilding, posing significant challenges and dilemmas for the role of international development. This speaks to a social contract model of post-conflict development whereby states provide core services (and security is now defined as a service alongside health, education, sanitation or the rule of law) to its people in a functioning government and administration. The other side of the contract is that people need to be able to hold their governments and leaders to account and to engage as citizens in the post-conflict state. This requires the strengthening of civil society organisations and state–civil society relations, as well as civilian oversight of governmental processes and institutions.

What its critics term the 'liberal peace' in the form of present-century peace operations in a range of settings was changed by the US invasion of Iraq in the face of much opposition, not least within the West. The invasion of Iraq reframed Afghanistan as a similar insurgency situation when indeed the initial military intervention in 2001 was supported by the UN Security Council and many UN member states in the aftermath of the 9/11 attacks in New York. International goodwill was squandered on Iraq to the detriment of any future arguments for humanitarian intervention or responsibility to protect in situations where there is threat of genocide or evidence of large-scale human rights abuses (Williams 2006; Sisk 2008).

The relationship between development, military presence and diplomacy has changed over the past decade. International responses to conflict in Iraq and Afghanistan have changed the context of action significantly. One revealing development has been the setting up of provincial reconstruction teams (PRTs) as civil–military multi-disciplinary teams to work in highly insecure areas in Afghanistan on related security, governance and development tasks and projects. They first became operational in 2002 and there are currently some 23 Coalition- and ISAF-managed teams. Humanitarian actors in particular do not welcome the civil-military ethos and structure of PRTs, revisiting their unease at the 'new humanitarianism' mentioned in Chapter 4. They view the PRTs as reducing the humanitarian space in wars with no front-line, compromising the humanitarian principles of impartiality and neutrality and going against well-established guidelines and codes of conduct on humanitarian assistance – including those prepared by the Red Cross and the UN Office for the Coordination of Humanitarian Affairs (Gordon 2010; Runge 2009).

Another development in Afghanistan and Iraq has been counter-insurgency tactics and operations that go beyond the 'integrated approach' involving military, diplomatic and development organisations highlighted in Chapter 4. 'Hearts and minds' campaigns cannot be equated with development projects and approaches and neither can development hope to protect itself with flags and emblems; the regular targeting of aid workers for kidnap and killing, and the bombing of the UN headquarters in Baghdad in 2003, are stark reminders of the collapse of any boundaries between war and development. As Howell (2006: 129–30) observes,

> Military personnel have appropriated the language of development, civil society and rights to dilute their militarism and to gain support locally. This strategy of 'hearts and minds' has taken

various forms such as handing out sweets to children on the streets, distributing leaflets portraying the enemy in a negative way, building schools, hospitals and wells, and delivering food aid.

One suggestion by Howell (2006: 131) is the need for humanitarian and development NGOs to consider becoming 'nationless', thus 'asserting greater control over the construction of their own identities'. Yet humanitarian and development interests now constitute a global power and industry in their own right and so should not be seen as victims of circumstance in the struggles for meaning and action on conflict and development; there is money to be mobilised by conflict-related programming, as indicated in Beall et al. (2006). During 2008, aid flows to 43 listed fragile and conflict-affected countries totalled US$33.2 billion, some 30 per cent of global ODA; over 50 per cent of this was allocated to six countries (in descending order: Afghanistan, Ethiopia, Iraq, West Bank and Gaza, Sudan and Uganda). ODA-related security activities rose from US$974 million in 2007 to US$1.5 billion in 2008 – mainly on peacebuilding, conflict prevention and resolution (OECD DAC 2010a).[2]

And not all soldiers are stereotypes, either; while counter-insurgency is certainly a part of the Afghan landscape and soldiers are there to stabilise and secure territory and confront the Taliban, they are also undertaking tasks that go beyond their conventional remit. The civil–military transfusion flows both ways. The implications and impact of increasingly civilian duties and contacts undertaken by soldiers present an issue that requires greater reflection. Peacekeepers have come under fire, too, for failures of protection and the abuse of authority. This also has to be addressed and put in the context of a long history of peacekeeping where many populations see them as the only real response of the outside world to their plight – when they failed to turn up, notably in Rwanda, their absence was not forgotten. There is a need for more shades of grey in debates about the interactions of the different actors on the ground.

This Afghanisation of international responses is beginning to reveal itself in international and bilateral organisations. Staff who have served in Afghanistan, and perhaps won promotion there, are now being given charge of regional or global aid and conflict portfolios in other parts of the world. There they face different challenges, not least cultural, and if these are not to become excuses for inaction or the inappropriate application of the Afghan lessons, they have to be understood and discussed with some humility. The consensus that is now in place on 'conflict and fragility' as a catch-all term for a myriad of conflict and post-conflict situations ranging from Azerbaijan to Zimbabwe – with Afghanistan, Iraq and Sudan in between – needs to be filtered through a rigorous process of analysis and understanding if it is to inform policies and programmes in very different contexts.

The quality of peace[3]

There is a certain paradox in the evolution of 'peacebuilding' as a policy watchword to guide international interventions given its alternative (and some would say primary) origins as a grassroots concept intertwined with conflict resolution. Conflict resolution aims to prevent, bring an end to, and transform violent conflict. Its immediate aim is to end hostilities where they have broken out or to prevent escalation of a dispute to the point where hostilities will break out and widespread violence and death will occur. The underlying aim of conflict *resolution* is to address the *root causes* of conflict, such as discrimination against minority groups, and to put in place an institutional and enabling environment for peace to ensure that violence will not break out or recur. The institutional architecture and norms around international conflict can be traced back to the founding of the United Nations in 1945, notably Chapter VI of the UN Charter with a focus on Pacific

Settlement of Disputes. Article 33 outlines the range of actions including 'negotiation, enquiry, mediation, conciliation, arbitration, judicial settlement, resort to regional agencies or arrangements, or other peaceful means of their own choice'. It also includes the 'good offices' (diplomacy) of the UN Secretary-General or Envoys. In terms of 'An Agenda for Peace' (Boutros-Ghali 1992), peacemaking efforts can be pre-emptive or *preventive* of conflict before it erupts: that is, preventive diplomacy. This emphasis on resolution has very strong foundations in religious, cultural and civil peace organisations that have promoted 'peacebuilding from below' stretching back through time.

Some argue that conflict resolution is a distinct undertaking that needs to be free of development structures and technocracy. Simon Fisher and Lada Zimina (2009) distinguish between 'technical' and 'transformative' peacebuilding – the former being the preserve of the 'peace industry' (including the expertise developed in the institutions discussed in Chapter 4) and the latter being driven by social movements – and argue for conflict transformation as the objective of peacebuilding and the key factor determining the quality of the peace being sought.

Kenneth Bush (the advocate of PCIA, cited in Chapter 3) considers the indigenous nature of peacebuilding to be the defining feature of the quality of the peace.

> It should be underscored that peacebuilding is not about the imposition of 'solutions', it is about the creation of opportunities, and the creation of political, economic, and social spaces, within which indigenous actors can identify, develop, and employ the resources necessary to build a peaceful, prosperous, and just society. Peacebuilding is a two-fold process requiring both the deconstruction of the structures of violence and the construction of the structures of peace. (Bush 1998: 33)

Bottom-up peacebuilding can also be seen by activists and groups as a way of holding donor and post-conflict governments and international and regional organisations to account as peacebuilding moves from rhetoric to practice. The DFID embrace of 'positive peace', for example, deserves closer scrutiny. How does it translate in practice? And are governments the only or best-suited agents to support and enable genuine positive change?

In the light of 'governance alternatives' discussed above, and the matter of whose security is being assured, the issue of accountability obviously arises. The notion of the social contract between government and citizen, state and society, is central to the globally dominant statebuilding/peacebuilding nexus. Much emphasis is placed on the ability of people to claim rights and services from their governments, and to have the means of holding their leaders to account. This focus on elite governance, at the centre of the state in the provision of services, is according to Richmond (2008a; 2008b) a 'virtual peace' and not really peace at all. Richmond and Franks (2009: 86) consider that success in terms of peace must be posed as some type of 'self-sustaining situation'. In order for this to be the case the harnessing of accountability is not only a matter of national governance but also international governance and legitimacy – where those who intervene are accountable to the people on whose behalf they claim to act. This too affects the quality of peace.

Conclusion

The use of development aid as an instrument of foreign policy in pursuit of political and/or military security objectives, beyond any stated or intended moral or altruistic motives, is not new. What is new is the alignment of aid with shifting notions of security in complex contemporary wars, and within complex international responses that have increasingly professionalised and rendered technocratic the nature and outcomes of development assistance in war-torn countries. The institutionalisation of conflict-related aid has to some extent made it more mobile and flexible (no longer waiting in the wings but now engaged in 'transition' from relief and supporting 'early recovery') in terms of timing and deployment in situations of ongoing or post-conflict violence. However, critics point to the need to understand and engage local people, society and institutions, to consider alternative forms of governance beyond and beneath the state in the search for stability and peace, and to promote more open debate on the politics of aid and security.

The shifting normative and policy parameters of international responses to protracted conflict in the Global South towards the recent discourses of statebuilding, peacebuilding and counter-insurgency mean that aid as a resource and normative aim in its own right has become subject to dominant and different objectives of intervention (stabilisation, counter-terrorism, fighting organised crime, preventing migration). This potentially compromises the moral foundations and justifications for aid.

Yet it can also be argued that the dilemmas of aid policy and programmes in conflict zones mirror the larger dilemma of how best to respond to contemporary conflicts. What outcomes are realistic for international interventions and likely to be supported by a more cynical tax-paying global public? How can support be provided to what works, even when it does not fit the models being promoted? How can conflict transformation rather than conflict management or 'do no harm' become more central to the relationship of conflict and development? And indeed, should it be central to that relationship?

Yet defining all interventions as part of some neo-liberal imperial project oversimplifies the causes, drivers and impact of conflict in many regions, as well as the challenging prospects for reducing violence and promoting any form of peace – negative or positive. Structural critiques endure with some merit on the ambition and failures of late twentieth-century international peace operations, but the scathing nature of such critiques can often overstate the extent to which these concerns tip over into 'neo-imperialism' or some form of neo-liberal conspiracy. Rather than understanding and addressing the failures or examining the intentions of international engagement in conflict situations, the overreach of development has simply been abandoned. No feasible alternatives are offered or studied.

Asymmetrical warfare[4] is part of that complex picture; so is growing militancy and terrorism as a form of violence, and the counter-terrorism to prevent and fight it; but so too are corrupt governments, and an aid industry defined as much by the prolif-eration of international NGOs arriving in disaster zones as it is by the technocracy of the UN. It remains an imperfect world. It may be that development is charged with being the 'intellectual handmaiden' of the status quo and a bulwark for neo-liberal adventurism in international conflicts – and yet the ideas and pro-grammes discussed here also reveal a radical agenda of change, one that does not accept conflict as inherent and seeks instead to transform the causes and courses of conflicts at many different points. Mistakes have been made and the real failure may be overreach in advancing this agenda for conflict prevention and peacebuilding through development policies and programmes, but it does not necessarily follow that the aim itself should be abandoned.

The potential directions that emerge from the debates and issues outlined here as the conflict and development agenda include suspending aid and realigning domestic budgets accord-ingly, scaling back the ambitions of all international efforts, and enabling global civil society to take more of a lead on peace and development issues. The nature of this debate is important, as there is a need to reconsider the role of development in conflict situations and to find ways through the polarising tendencies of current debates if responding to international conflict is to remain a global concern. This requires some humility on the part of both academics and practitioners in learning from the post-Cold War experience and reconsidering the main questions. What international objectives, resources and outcomes can feasibly be expected and pursued? And how best can national governments and societies in conflict-affected countries be supported in shaping their own visions and efforts for something called peace and something called development?

Notes

Chapter 1

1   The reference to the Global South refers to the G77 membership of 130 countries. However, that listing includes exceptions to the conflict and development agenda (China, for example) and omits some pertinent cases (such as Central Asia, including Kyrgyzstan).

2   The five permanent members (P5) of the Security Council are Russia, China, the United States, the United Kingdom and France. There is a rotating system of a further ten non-permanent members elected for two-year terms by the General Assembly. The P5 system reflects the post-Second World War consensus and has been subject to increasing calls for reform to reflect shifts in global power and to accord states such as India, Brazil, South Africa, Germany and Japan more influence. In fact, recent elections to the Security Council in 2010 have for the first time provided a full Security Council where all these countries are members, indicating that at last action for reform may be possible.

3   Liberal peace emerges as a challenge to the conservative realist thinking that dominated the Cold War period in terms of the search for a 'balance of power' in an assumed anarchical international setting of contending national interests. Yet distinctions among liberals emerge in terms of shades of liberal pacifism (Schumpeter's views on capitalist democracy as avoiding wars), liberal imperialism (Machiavellian ideas of an armed and expanding republic finding glory and defending its status) and liberal internationalism (Kant's ideas taken up here) that embrace a range of views and policies that move from left to right (Doyle 2004).

4   Bilateral aid refers to development assistance provided by govern-
    ments directly to another country, while multilateral aid refers to
    government aid that is provided to other countries through interna-
    tional organisations such as the UN, the World Bank and to some
    extent the European Commission.

5   Counting the costs of war is a controversial area of academic
    research and an important parameter for policymaking in under-
    standing the trends and impacts of conflict to shape humanitarian,
    peacekeeping and other responses. We do not know if responses are
    working if we cannot analyse trends based on credible data.
    Notable repositories of extensive databases and analysis that drive
    this work include the University of Uppsala Conflict Data Project
    (UCDP, Sweden), the Centre for the Study of Civil War at PRIO
    (CSCW, International Peace Research Institute Oslo, Norway), the
    Correlates of War Project originally at the University of Michigan
    and now at Penn State (US), the Minorities at Risk project at the
    University of Maryland (US), the Strategic Foresight Group
    (Mumbai, India), and the Human Security Report Project at the
    University of British Colombia (Canada) . The UCDP threshold of
    more than 25 battle-related deaths in one year is a widely-used
    international used measure of 'armed conflict'. A 'major armed
    conflict' or 'war' is referred to as more than 1000 battle-related
    deaths in one year. UCDP focuses on state-based conflict, that is,
    where at least one of the parties to the conflict a government (SIPRI
    2010, Harbom and Wallensteen 2010). However, in understanding
    contemporary wars, the restrictions and challenges of counting
    battle-deaths make it a narrow measure of the dynamics and impact
    (direct and indirect) of what is often chronic violence, displacement,
    dispersed targeted fighting, lost livelihoods and destruction of func-
    tioning government, society and economy. The Human Security
    Report Project (2005, 2006) has sought to also track non state-
    based conflict that is, involving militias, guerrillas, warlords, clans
    and communal groups but not a government. This exercise is also
    beset by data-gathering problems in conflict-affected areas and so
    data overall is improving and indicative of overall trends but
    remains work in progress. Box 1 provides a statistical overview of

current global conflict trends with a focus on implications for development. Cramer (2006, Chapter 2) provides an excellent review of the methodologies and limitations of costing violent conflict. There has been recent controversy about the methodology of tracking direct and indirect deaths from war and conflict, and the mythological status of some statistics, notably the oft- cited 'fact' that 90% of victims of war are civilian. For more on this see Obermayer et al (2008), Spagat et al. (2009) and Roberts (2010).

6   This figure is based on an ALNAP study (2010) that sought to align different methods to arrive at a figure of US$7 billion for total humanitarian flows to emergencies from public and private sources in 2008. GHA (2010) is a well-cited source and gives a much higher estimate of US$15.1billion. However, this figure includes estimated flows from state, non-state and private funding as well as post-conflict assistance.

7   ODA refers to Official Development Assistance from governments and includes both development and humanitarian aid. Interestingly, the OECD DAC analysis of the 2009 figures finds that there is 'additional aid of US$27 billion from 2004 to 2010, but a US$21 billion shortfall between what donors promised in 2005 [0.7 per cent of GNI] and the OECD estimates for the 2010 outcome. Of this shortfall, US$17 billion is the result of lower-than-promised giving by the donors and US$4 billion is the result of lower-than-expected GNI because of the economic crisis.' <http://www.oecd.org/document/20/0,3343,en_21571361_44315115_44617556_1_1_1_1,00.html> (2 November 2010).

8   For summaries of these schools of thought in International Relations see, inter alia, Dunne, Kurki and Smith (2010) and Jackson and Sørensen (2010); and in Development Studies Desai and Potter (2002), Kothari (2005a) and Rist (2008). Richmond (2008a; 2008b) provides an analysis and typology of ways in which peace has been understood by different strands of International Relations theory.

9   The evolution of the concept of human security through the 1990s was significant in advocating that international development respond not only to basic human needs but to human needs as

related to security, beyond survival. This was framed as 'freedom from want' and 'freedom from fear'. Human security is discussed in more detail in Chapter 5. Feminist critical studies have also contributed to this destabilising of the state and conventional notions of security to question the core theoretical and practical focus of the security agenda and how far it is gendered and arises from flawed assumptions about state, society and security (Chapter 4 will deal more with this). For more on the evolution of security studies see Booth (2004); Buzan and Hansen (2009); and Williams (2008).

10   For a classic conceptual analysis of the respective roles, commonalities and differences among conflict researchers, peace researchers and strategists, see Groom (1988).

11   For an overview of the field see Barash and Webel (2009); Crocker, Hampson and Aall (2001); Galtung (1985); Jacoby (2008); Jeong (2000; 2008); Mack and Synder (1957); Ramsbotham, Woodhouse and Miall (2005); Rogers and Ramsbotham (1999).

12   These are eight development targets set by the international community at the 2000 Millennium Summit, to be achieved by 2015. They include halving poverty, increasing access to primary education, and reducing child mortality. See <http://www.un.org/millenniumgoals/> (accessed 1 November 2010).

13   This framing of how development relates to conflict arises from considerations of conflict resolution and seeking lasting change and transformation of the causes and dynamics of conflict rather than palliative approaches. It can be found, for example, in the Quaker-inspired work of Simon Fisher (2000) on 'responding to conflict', and is also well discussed by Jonathan Goodhand (2001: 30–3).

Chapter 2

1   See Anderson (1991); Brown (2001); Calhoun (2007); Gellner (1983); Kedourie (1993); Smith (1991; 1993).

2   The notion of trusteeship comes from the Trusteeship Council of the UN, a body that had been considered defunct by the 1990s; it had

been set up in 1945 as part of the decolonisation process that would support ungoverned territories and provide an international framework of government as these entities prepared for independence. Ironically, one of graduates of trusteeship was the former Italian-controlled Somaliland.

3   A critical discussion of the literature on revolutions is beyond the scope of this chapter. However, the drive to understand the revolutions that defined an era of decolonisation and Cold War superpower geopolitics spawned a literature on revolutionary wars ranging across Zimbabwe, Mozambique, Algeria, and Vietnam as well as the post-revolution regimes of China and Russia. Debates raged about theoretical frameworks, research methodologies and ideology. The structure and agency debate was one that persisted in terms of whether peasants revolt because they feel and express grievances in concrete terms of land tenure, markets and a way of life, or whether systemic factors such as the class system itself and centre–periphery global structures determine the likelihood of violence.

4   This creation and denigration of 'otherness' is resonant with Johan Galtung's notion of 'cultural violence', where use of symbols and stereotyping forges suspicion, fear and hatred, and in so doing becomes a source for other forms of direct and structural violence (Galtung 1990).

5   The only grievance-related variable that might have a place in this model is the characteristic of 'ethnic dominance', whereby the society has one large ethnic group that makes up 45–90 per cent of the population. This challenge to minority rights, they argue, has some salience in defining the likelihood of conflict.

Chapter 3

1   This is the basic map on which the dynamics – how these factors are interacting – as well as key actors and their motivations are explored and mapped to provide scenarios for conflict. Positive

   drivers for peace and stability would be identified in the fuller assessment.

2   A programme refers to a set of connected and planned projects that are implemented under an overall umbrella strategy that shapes the programme. A project is one component of an overall programme, or may be a discrete stand-alone initiative.

3   For an overall discussion on the debates surrounding PCIA, see the interesting dialogues facilitated by the Berghof Foundation in 2003, <http://www.berghof-handbook.net/>

Chapter 4

1   Within this, the humanitarian and development communities reflect distinct organisational and even ideational cultures that have played out in policy and practice in responding to conflict. They have come together with necessary tension and mixed results. First, *humanitarian intervention* has emerged as a contested paradigm for international responses to violent conflict involving large-scale human rights abuses within a sovereign state where the government may or may not exist, or has abdicated its responsibility to protect its citizens and thus become part of the problem rather than the solution. Second, the strategy of *linking relief and development* has emerged as part of a growing recognition that violent conflicts do not simply end – a reality that undermines institutional divisions of labour in a sequenced timeline of war and emergency humanitarian assistance followed at some point by the restoration of peace and the implementation of long-term sustainable development programmes. Extended complex emergencies meant that humanitarian aid was being continued while at the same time development actors were becoming engaged at an earlier juncture to 'bridge the gap' between relief and development in the form of transitional or early-recovery programmes. Boundaries between humanitarian and development assistance are very blurred in conflict-related programming. Both types of aid are featured here in discussing policies and programmes in conflict-affected areas. Humanitarian aid refers to

emergency, immediate, life-saving actions historically guided by principles of neutrality and impartiality, while development assistance is more long-term and includes sustainable approaches to poverty alleviation and governance that in recent times have been framed within the global framework of the MDGs.

2   It should be noted that the continuum is not necessarily linear, though programmes have been criticised for making such an assumption. Any of these actions are in themselves complex and caught up with the dynamics of conflict and peace in any situation.

3   For more on humanitarian intervention, including detailed case studies, see Moore (1998), Ramsbotham and Woodhouse (1996), Weiss (2007) and Wheeler (2002). On new humanitarianism see Fox (2001), Macrae (2002) and Woodward (2001).

4   For a comprehensive and critical review of early warning systems see Nyheim (2008). For more on the provenance of conflict prevention as concept and approach see Aall (2004), Carnegie Commission on Preventing Deadly Conflict (1997), Hamburg (2002) and Hampson and Malone (2002).

5   See UN 2005 World Summit Outcome (A/60/L.1), paras 97–105, <http://daccess-dds-y.un.org/doc/UNDOC/GEN/N05/487/60/PDF/ N0548760.pdf?OpenElement> (accessed 15 December 2010); and UN Security Council Resolution 1645 (2005), <http://daccess-dds-y.un.org/doc/UNDOC/GEN/N05/654/17/PDF/N0565417.pdf? OpenElement> (accessed 15 December 2010).

6   Taken from UN SCR 1645 (2005).

7   In fact, the nature and structure of the state – including conditions of weak and collapsed states – has academic roots in political science and the study of democracy and democratisation. Elements of this are discussed in Chapter 6. The object here is simply to outline the engagement of recent donor policy development trends with fragile states and statebuilding.

8   See, for example, IDS (2010) and Leftwich (2000).

9   See OECD DAC (2004). A 2007 OECD DAC handbook on security system reform builds on these guidelines. See <www.oecd.org/ dataoecd/43/25/38406485.pdf> (accessed 20 December 2010).

Chapter 5

1   For more on the field of gender and development see Boserup (1970), Cornwall, Harrison and Whitehead (2007), Elson (1991), Jackson and Pearson (1998), Kabeer (1994) and Moser (1991; 1993).

2   For an overview of Feminist International Relations see Enloe (1989; 2007), Grant and Newland (1991), Peterson (1992), Peterson and Runyan (1993), Pettman (1996), Shepherd (2010) and Tickner (1992; 2001).

3   For an overview of 'women and war' feminist approaches and issues see Boulding (2000), Brownmiller (1976), Burguieres (1990), Cockburn and Zarkov (2002), Cohn and Enloe (2003), Elshtain (1995), Enloe (1988; 1989; 2007), Jacobs, Jacobson and Marchbank (2000), Meintjes, Turshen and Pillay (2001), Molyneux (1985), Moser and Clark (2001) and O' Gorman (1999).

4   See, for example, Sjoberg and Gentry (2007).

5   See, for example, Al-Ali and Pratt (2009) and Enloe (2007).

6   See, for example, Naraghi-Anderlini (2007).

7   This policy work includes International Committee of the Red Cross (ICRC 2001), Rehn and Johnson Sirleaf (2002), United Nations (2002), International Alert (2002) and Sherriff with Barnes (2008).

8   For an earlier and extended discussion of these themes see O' Gorman (1999).

9   The term 'struggles in the struggle' is taken from Norman Kriger's 1992 work on *Zimbabwe's Guerrilla War: Peasant Voices*, where she unearths agendas other than nationalism to explain peasant mobilisation for revolution. These agendas include gender, generation and social stratification.

10 For further perspectives on masculinity, war, violence and international relations see Cockburn and Zarkov (2002), Parpart and Zalewski (2008) and Pettman (1996: Chapter 5).

11 United Nations Security Council (2000), Rehn and Johnson Sirleaf (2002), and United Nations (2004).

12 For the use of this term see International Crisis Group (2008).

13 For examples from Oxfam see O' Connell (1993); Walker (1994); for the Bridge project see Byrne (1995) and El Jack (2003); for ACORD see El Bushra and Piza-Lopez (1993); and for International Alert see El Bushra (2003) and Naraghi-Anderlini (2001).

14 This is considered the benchmark for international aid policy and programming on security sector governance in situations of conflict and fragility. The original Handbook was completed in 2007 and it is due to advocacy and attention from some members of the DAC as well as civil society organisations that the gender chapter was later developed in line with UNSCR 1325.

15 <http://www.un.org/en/peacekeeping/documents/factsheet.pdf> (accessed 10 July 2010).

16 <http://www.un.org/en/peacekeeping/contributors/gender.shtml> (accessed 10 July 2010).

17 In response to the revelations and emergence of sexual exploitation and abuse (SEA) as an issue since the early 1990s, UN, NGO and donor policies and frameworks are increasingly signing up to different codes of conduct for operating in crisis and post-crisis situations. The 1994 'Code of Conduct for the International Red Cross and Red Crescent Movement and NGOs in Disaster Relief' is a widely accepted basis for conduct in the delivery of humanitarian assistance. There is also the 2006 'Statement of Commitment on Eliminating Sexual Exploitation and Abuse by UN and non-UN Personnel', and the Humanitarian Accountability Partnership (HAP); the latter works with humanitarian NGOs to make confidential reporting arrangements for beneficiaries and encourage peer review and support when addressing the risks of SEA in the delivery of humanitarian assistance and enforcing accountability at all levels.

Chapter 6

1 ICG (2006); UN (2006a); UN (2006b).
2 These are the aid figures for the 79 member states of the OECD's Development Assistance Committee.

3   This term features in Richmond and MacGinty (2007).

4   Asymmetric warfare refers to the disparity of strong and weak pro-
tagonists, whereby the perceived weaker side in terms of conventional power and military resources wages war with different (often
indirect) tactics that typically implicate and affect civilians. As a
result, the weaker actor may in fact wield greater power or gain
victories at the expense of the apparently greater military strength
of the opponent. These tactics of asymmetric warfare are often associated with guerrilla wars and insurgency, and the counter-
insurgency tactics developed by more conventional forces to
respond to them. Most recently there have been debates about the
extent to which terrorism has become an influential form of asymmetric warfare. See Mack (1975) and Stepanova (2008).

Bibliography

Aall, P. (2004) 'Non-Governmental Organisations and Conflict Prevention: Roles, Capabilities, Limitations' in D. Carment and A. Schnabel
(eds), *Conflict Prevention: from Rhetoric to Reality*, Lexington
Books, Boston MA.

Abirafeh, L. (2009) *Gender and International Aid in Afghanistan: the
Politics and Effects of Intervention*, McFarland and Company,
Jefferson NC and London.

Adams, M. and M. Bradbury (1995) 'Conflict and Development: Organ-
isational Adaptation in Conflict Situations', Oxfam Working Paper,
Oxfam UK and Ireland with ACORD, Responding to Conflict
(RTC) and University of Birmingham.

Agerbak, L. (1992) 'Breaking the Cycle of Violence: Doing Development
in Situations of Conflict', *Development in Practice* 1 (3): 151–8.

Al-Ali, N. and N. Pratt (2009) *What Kind of Liberation? Women and the
Occupation of Iraq*, University of California Press, Berkeley CA.

Allen, E. et al. (1978) 'Against Sociobiology' in A. L. Kaplan (ed.), *The
Sociobiology Debate: Readings on Ethical and Scientific Issues*,
Harper and Row Publishers, New York NY.

ALNAP (2010) 'The State of Humanitarian Assistance: Assessing
Performance and Progress', pilot study, ALNAP at ODI, London.

Amnesty International (2008) 'Liberia: a Flawed Process Discriminates
against Women and Girls' (AFR 34/ 004/ 2008), Amnesty International, London. <http://www.amnesty.ca/amnestynews/ upload/
AFR34004 2008.pdf> (accessed 19 December 2010).

Anderson, B. (1991 [1983]) *Imagined Communities: Reflections on the
Origins and Spread of Nationalism*, second revised edition, Verso,
London.

Anderson, M. (1999) *Do No Harm: How Aid Can Support Peace – or*

War, Lynne Rienner, Boulder CO and London.

Atwood, D. and F. Tanner (2007) 'The UN Peacebuilding Commission and International Geneva', *Disarmament Forum* 2: 22–36.

Ayoob, M. (2001) 'State Making, State Breaking, and State Failure' in C. Crocker, F. O. Hampson and P. Aall (eds), *Turbulent Peace*, USIP Press, Washington DC.

Bannon, I. and M. Correia (eds) (2006) *The Other Half of Gender: Men's Issues in Development*, World Bank, Washington.

Barash, D. P. and C. Webel (2009) *Peace and Conflict Studies*, second edition, Sage, London.

Barbolet, A., R. Goldwyn, H. Groenewald and A. Sherriff (2005) 'The Utility and Dilemmas of Conflict Sensitivity' in D. Bloomfield, M. Fischer and B. Schmelzle (eds), *New Trends in Peace and Conflict Impact Assessment (PCIA)* (Berghof Handbook Dialogue Series No. 4), Berghof Research Centre for Constructive Conflict Management, Berlin, pp. 2–17. <http://www.berghof-handbook. net/documents/publications/dialogue4_barbolet_etal.pdf> (accessed 14 October 2010).

Barnett, J. (2008) 'Peace and Development: Towards a New Synthesis', *Journal of Peace Research* 45 (1): 75–89.

Beall, J., T. Goodfellow and J. Putzel (2006) 'The Discourse of Terrorism, Security and Development', *Journal of International Development* 18 (1): 51–67.

Bellamy, A. J. (2009) *A Responsibility to Protect: the Global Effort to End Mass Atrocities*, Polity Press, Cambridge.

Berdal, M. (2005) 'Beyond Greed and Grievance – and Not Too Soon ...', review essay, *Review of International Studies* 31 (4): 687–98.

Berdal M. and D. M. Malone (eds) (2000) *Greed and Grievance: Economic Agendas in Civil Wars*, Lynne Rienner, Boulder CO.

Booth, K. (ed.) (2004) *Critical Security Studies and World Politics*, Lynne Rienner, Boulder CO.

Boserup, E. (1970) *Woman's Role in Economic Development* (1989 edition), Earthscan, London.

Boulding, E. (2000) *Cultures of Peace: the Hidden Side of History*, Syracuse University Press, Syracuse NY.

Boutros-Ghali, B. (1992) 'An Agenda for Peace: Preventive Diplomacy, Peacemaking and Peacekeeping', Secretary-General's Report, United

Nations, New York NY.

—— (1995) 'An Agenda for Development', Secretary-General's Report, United Nations, New York NY.

Bradbury, M. (2008) *Becoming Somaliland*, James Currey, Oxford.

Brown, M. E. (2001) 'Ethnic and Internal Conflicts: Causes and Implications' in C. Crocker et al. (eds) (2001) *Turbulent Peace: the Challenges of Managing International Conflict* (2005 reprint), United States Institute of Peace, Washington DC, pp. 209–26.

Brownmiller, S. (1976) *Against Our Will: Men, Women and Rape*, Bantam, New York NY.

Buhaug, H., N. P. Gleditsch and O. M. Theisen (2008) 'Implications of Climate Change for Armed Conflict', report, PRIO and World Bank, Oslo and Washington DC. <http://siteresources.worldbank.org/INTRANETSOCIALDEVEL-OPMENT/Resources/SDCCWorkingPaper_Conflict.pdf> (accessed 13 October 2010).

Burguieres, M. (1990) 'Feminist Approaches to Peace: Another Step for Peace Studies', *Millennium* 19 (1): 1–18.

Bush, K. (1998) 'A Measure of Peace: Peace and Conflict Impact Assessment (PCIA) of Development Projects in Conflict Zones', Working Paper No. 1, Evaluation Unit, International Development Research Centre, Ottawa, Canada.

—— (2003) 'PCIA Five Years On: the Commodification of an Idea' in A. Austin, M. Fischer and O. Wils (eds), *Peace and Conflict Impact Assessment. Critical Views on Theory and Practice* (Berghof Handbook Dialogue Series No. 1), Berghof Research Centre for Constructive Conflict Management, Berlin, pp. 37–51. <http://www.berghof-handbook.net/documents/publications/dia-logue1_pcia_complete.pdf> (accessed 4 December 2010).

Buzan, B. and L. Hansen (eds) (2009) *The Evolution of International Security Studies*, Cambridge University Press, Cambridge.

Byrne, B. (1995) 'Gender, Conflict and Development, Volume 1: Overview', BRIDGE Report (Briefings on Development and Gender) No. 34, Sussex, Institute of Development Studies.

Calhoun, C. (2007) *Nations Matter: Culture, History and the Cosmopolitan Dream*, Routledge, Abingdon.

Carnegie Commission on Preventing Deadly Conflict (1997) 'Preventing

Deadly Conflict', Final Report, Carnegie Corporation, New York. <http://www.wilsoncenter.org/subsites/ccpdc/pubs/rept97/finfr.htm> (accessed 2 November 2010).

Chandler, D. (2004) 'The Responsibility to Protect: Imposing the Liberal Peace', *International Peacekeeping* 11 (1): 59–81.

—— (2010) 'The Uncritical Critique of Liberal Peace', *Review of International Studies*, Cambridge Journals Online, doi:10.1017/5026021051000823 (accessed 26 August 2010).

Chapman, N., D. Duncan, D. Timberman and K. Abeygunawardana (2009) 'Evaluation of Donor-Supported Activities in Conflict-Sensitive Development and Conflict Prevention and Peacebuilding in Sri Lanka', Main Evaluation Report, testing of OECD DAC pilot guidance for monitoring and evaluation of conflict prevention and peacebuilding, OECD, Paris. <http://www.oecd.org/dataoecd/63/50/44138006.pdf>.

Chopra, J. (2002) 'Building State Failure in East Timor', *Development and Change* 33 (5): 679–1000.

Cockburn, C. and Z. Zarkov (eds) (2002) *The Postwar Moment: Militaries, Masculinities and International Peacekeeping*, Lawrence and Wishart, London.

Cohn, C. and C. Enloe (2003) 'A Conversation with Cynthia Enloe: Feminists Look at Masculinity and Men Who Wage War', Signs 24 (4): 1187–1207.

Cohn, C., H. Kinsella and S. Gibbings (2004), 'Women, Peace and Security: Resolution 1325', *International Feminist Journal of Politics* 6 (1): 130–40.

Collier, P. (2001) 'Economic Causes of Civil Conflict and Their Implications for Policy', in C. Crocker, F. O. Hampson and P. Aall (eds), *Turbulent Peace: The Challenges of Managing International Conflict* (reprinted 2005), United States Institute of Peace, Washington DC.

—— (2008) 'The Conflict Trap' in *The Bottom Billion: Why the Poorest Countries are Failing and What Can be Done About It*, Oxford University Press, Oxford, Chapter 2, pp. 17–37.

Collier, P. and A. Hoeffler (2000) 'Greed and Grievance in Civil War', Policy Research Working Paper 2355, World Bank, Washington DC.

Connell, R. W. (2000) *The Men and the Boys*, Polity Press, Cambridge.

—— (2002) 'Masculinities, the Reduction of Violence and the Pursuit of Peace' in C. Cockburn and D. Zarkov (eds) *The Postwar Moment: Militaries, Masculinities and International Peacekeeping*, Lawrence and Wishart, London.

Cooper, N. (2005) 'Picking out the Pieces of the Liberal Peace', *Security Dialogue* 36 (4): 463–78.

Cooper, R. (2003) *The Breaking of Nations: Order and Chaos in the Twenty-First Century*, Atlantic Monthly Press, New York NY.

Cornwall, A., E. Harrison and A. Whitehead (2007) *Feminisms in Development: Contradictions, Contestations and Challenges*, Zed Books, London and New York NY.

Coser, L. (1956) *The Functions of Social Conflict*, The Free Press, New York NY.

Cramer, C. (2002) 'Homo Economicus Goes to War: Methodological Individualism, Rational Choice, and the Political Economy of War', *World Development* 30 (11): 1845–64.

—— (2003) 'Does Inequality Cause Conflict?', *Journal of International Development* 15 (4): 397–412.

—— (2006) *Civil War Is Not a Stupid Thing: Accounting for Violence in Developing Countries*, Hurst and Company, London.

—— (2010) 'What Price Peace? Working Paper 1: Methodological Challenges of Assessing Cost-Effectiveness of Conflict Prevention', unpublished study commissioned by DFID, UK, summary. <http://www.gsdrc.org/docs/open/HD702.pdf> (accessed 15 December 2010).

Crocker, C., F. O. Hampson and P. Aall (eds) (2001) *Turbulent Peace: The Challenges of Managing International Conflict* (reprinted 2005), United States Institute of Peace, Washington DC.

Curle, A. (1971) *Making Peace*, London, Tavistock Publications.

Davies, J. C. (1980) 'Biological Perspectives on Human Conflict' in T. R. Gurr (ed.), *Handbook of Political Conflict*, The Free Press, New York NY, pp. 19–69.

Desai, V. and B. Potter (eds) (2002) *The Companion to Development Studies*. Arnold, London.

de Waal, A. (1997) *Famine Crimes: Politics and the Disaster Relief Industry in Africa*, African Rights and James Currey, London and Oxford.

—— (2009) 'Mission without End? Peacekeeping in the African Political Marketplace', *International Affairs* 85 (1): 99–113.

DFID (2002) 'Conducting Conflict Assessment: Guidance Notes', Department for International Development, London. <http://webarchive.nationalarchives.gov.uk/+/http://www.dfid.gov.uk/documents/publications/conflictassessmentguidance.pdf> (accessed 13 October 2010).

—— (2003) 'Summary of Evaluation of the Conflict Prevention Pools', Department for International Development, London. <http://dev-zone.cen.brad.ac.uk/acad/cics/publications/conflict prevention/conclusions/evaluation_summary_%28EV647%29.pdf> (accessed 5 December 2010).

—— (2009) 'Eliminating World Poverty: Building Our Common Future', government white paper, Department for International Development, London. <www.dfid.gov.uk/documents/white-paper/building-our-common-future-print.pdf> (accessed 20 December 2010).

—— (2010) 'Building Peaceful States and Societies: a DFID Practice Paper', DFID, London. <www.reliefweb.int/rw/lib.nsf/db900SID/JBRN-83GJC2?OpenDocument> (accessed 20 December 2010).

Dollard, J., N. E. Miller, L. W. Doob, O. H. Mowrer and R. S. Sears (1988 [1939]) *Frustration and Aggression*, Routledge, London (reprint).

Doyle, M. W. (1983a) 'Kant, Liberal Legacies and Freedom' (Part 1), *Philosophy and Public Affairs* 12 (3): 205–35.

—— (1983b) 'Kant, Liberal Legacies and Freedom' (Part 2), *Philosophy and Public Affairs* 12 (4): 323–53.

—— (2004) 'Liberal Internationalism: Peace, War and Democracy', Nobelprize.org, Official Website of the Nobel Prize, 22 June 2004. <http://nobelprize.org/nobel_prizes/peace/articles/doyle/> (accessed 10 November 2010).

Doyle, M. W. and N. Sambanis (2006) *Making War and Building Peace*, Princeton University Press, Princeton NJ.

Duffield, M. (2001) *Global Governance and New Wars: the Merging of Development and Security*, Zed Books, London.

—— (2007) *Development, Security and Unending War*, Polity, Cambridge.

Dunne, T., M. Kurki and S. Smith (eds) (2010) *International Relations Theories: Discipline and Diversity*, second edition, Oxford University Press, Oxford.

Easterly, W. (2006) *The White Man's Burden*, Oxford University Press, Oxford.

El Jack, A. (2003) 'Gender and Armed Conflict: Overview Report', BRIDGE (Briefings on Development and Gender), Institute of Development Studies University of Sussex.

El-Bushra, J. (2003) 'Women Building Peace: Sharing Know-How', workshop report, International Alert, London.

El-Bushra, J. and E. Piza-Lopez (1993) 'Development in Conflict: the Gender Dimension', workshop report, Oxfam/Agency for Cooperation and Research and Development (ACORD), Oxford.

Elshtain, J. B. (1995) *Women and War*, second edition, University of Chicago Press, Chicago IL.

Elson, D. (1991) *Male Bias in the Development Process*, Manchester University Press, Manchester.

Enloe, C. (1988) *Does Khaki Become You? The Militarization of Women's Lives*, second edition, Pandora Press, London.

—— (1989) *Bananas, Beaches and Bases: Making Feminist Sense of International Politics*, Pandora, London.

—— (2002) 'Demilitarization of More of the Same? Feminist Questions to Ask in the Postwar Moment' in C. Cockburn and D. Zarkov (eds), *The Postwar Moment: Militaries, Masculinities and International Peacekeeping*, Lawrence and Wishart, London.

—— (2007) *Globalization and Militarism: Feminists Make the Link*. Maryland: Rowan and Littlefield.

EU (2003) 'A Secure Europe in a Better World', document proposed by Javier Solana, High Representative for Common, Foreign and Security Policy (CFSP) and adopted at the European Council in Brussels, 12 December.

Evans, G. (2008) *The Responsibility to Protect: Ending Mass Atrocity Crimes Once and for All,* Brookings Institution Press, Washington DC.

Failed States Index (2009) Index prepared by the Fund for Peace and Foreign Policy magazine, Washington. <http://www.foreignpolicy.com/failedstates> (accessed 20 October 2010).

Fearon, J. and D. Laitin (2003) 'Ethnicity, Insurgency and Civil War', *American Political Science Review* 97 (1): 75–90.

Fisher, S. (ed.) (2000) *Working with Conflict: Skills and Strategies for Action*, Zed Books, London.

Fisher, S. and L. Zimina (2009) 'Just Wasting Our Time? Provocative Thoughts for Peacebuiders' in B. Schmelzle and M. Fischer (eds), *Peacebuilding at a Crossroads? Dilemmas and Paths for Another Generation* (Berghof Handbook Dialogue Series No. 7), Berghof Research Centre for Constructive Conflict Management, Berlin, pp. 11–35.

Fox, F. (2001) 'New Humanitarianism: Does It Provide a Moral Banner for the Twenty-First Century?' *Disasters* 24 (4): 275–89.

Galtung, J. (1969) 'Violence, Peace and Peace Research', *Journal of Peace Research* 6 (3): 167–91.

—— (1985) Twenty-Five Years of Peace Research: Ten Challenges and Some Responses, *Journal of Peace Research* 22 (2): 141–58.

—— (1990) 'Cultural Violence', *Journal of Peace Research* 23 (3): 291–305.

Gellner, E. (1983) *Nations and Nationalism*, Basil Blackwell, Oxford.

GHA (2010) 'GHA Report 2010', Global Humanitarian Assistance, Development Initiatives, Well, Somerset. <http://www.globalhumanitarianassistance.org/wp-content/uploads/2010/07/GHA_Report8.pdf> (accessed 2 November 2010).

Gleditsch, N. P. (1998) 'Armed Conflict and the Environment: a Critique of the Literature', *Journal of Peace Research* 35 (3): 381–400.

Glennie, J. (2008) *The Trouble with Aid: Why Less Would Mean More for Africa*, Zed Books, London.

Global Witness (1998) 'A Rough Trade: the Role of Governments and Companies in the Angolan Conflict', research report, Global Witness Ltd, London.

Goodhand, J. (2001) 'Violent Conflict, Poverty and Chronic Poverty', CPRC Working Paper 6, Chronic Poverty Research Centre, UK. <http://www.chronicpoverty.org/publications/details/violent-conflict-poverty-and-chronic-poverty/ss> (accessed 18 October 2010)

—— (2003) 'Enduring Disorder and Persistent Poverty: a Review of the Linkages between War and Chronic Poverty', *World Development* 31 (3): 629–46.

Gordon, S. (2010) 'The United Kingdom's Stabilisation Model and Afghanistan: the Impact on Humanitarian Actors', *Disasters* 34 (3): 368–87.

Gourevitch, P. (2010) 'Alms Dealers: Can You Provide Humanitarian Aid without Facilitating Conflicts?', *New Yorker*, 11 October 2010.

GPI (2009) 'Peace: Its Causes and Economic Value', discussion paper, Global Peace Index, Institute for Economics and Peace, Sydney.

—— (2010) 'Global Peace Index 2010', Institute for Economics and Peace, Sydney. <http://www.visionofhumanity.org/info-center/media-pack/2010-global-peace-index/> (accessed 28 October 2010).

Grant, R. and K. Newland (eds) (1991) *Gender and International Relations*, Open University Press, Buckingham.

Grindle, M. (2004) 'Good Enough Governance: Poverty Reduction and Reform in Developing Countries', *Governance: an International Journal of Policy, Administration, and Institutions* 17 (1): 525–48.

Groom, A. J. R. (1988) 'Paradigms in Conflict: the Strategist, the Conflict Researcher and the Peace Researcher', *Review of International Studies* 14 (2): 97–115.

Gsänger, H. and C. Feyen (2003) 'PCIA Methodology: a Development Practitioner's Perspective', in A. Austin, M. Fischer and O. Wils (eds), *Peace and Conflict Impact Assessment: Critical Views on Theory and Practice* (Berghof Handbook Dialogue Series No. 1), Berghof Research Centre for Constructive Conflict Management, Berlin, pp. 67–75. <http://www.berghof-handbook.net/documents/publications/dialogue1_pcia_complete.pdf> (accessed 4 December 2010).

GTZ (2008) 'Peace and Conflict Assessment: a Methodological Framework for Conflict- and Peace-Oriented Alignment of Development Programmes', Gesellschaft für Technische Zusammenarbeit (GTZ) for the German Federal Ministry for Economic Cooperation and Development (BMZ), Eschborn, Germany. <http://www2.gtz.de/dokumente/bib/gtz2008-0381en-crisis-pca.pdf> (accessed 14 October 2010).

Gurr, T. (1970) *Why Men Rebel*, Princeton University Press, Princeton NJ.

Hamburg, D. A. (2002) *No More Killing Fields: Preventing Deadly Conflict*, Rowman and Littlefield, New York NY.

Hampson, F. O. and D. M. Malone (eds) (2002) *From Reaction of Conflict Prevention: Opportunities for the UN System*, Lynne Rienner, Boulder CO.

Hanlon, J. (2006) '200 Wars and the Humanitarian Response', in H. Yanacopulos and J. Hanlon (eds), *Civil War, Civil Peace*, Open University and James Currey, Milton Keynes and Oxford.

Harbom, L. and P. Wallensteen (2009) 'Armed Conflicts, 1946–2008', *Journal of Peace Research* 46 (4): 477–87.

—— (2010) 'Armed Conflict, 1946–2009', *Journal of Peace Research* 47 (4): 501–10.

Hettne, B. (1983) 'Peace and Development: Contradictions and Compatibilities,' *Journal of Peace Research* 20 (4): 329–42.

Hoffman, M. (2003) 'PCIA Methodology: Evolving Art Form or Practical Dead End' in A. Austin, M. Fischer and O. Wils (eds), *Peace and Conflict Impact Assessment. Critical Views on Theory and Practice* (Berghof Handbook Dialogue Series No. 1), Berghof Research Centre for Constructive Conflict Management, Berlin, pp. 11–35. <http://www.berghof-handbook.net/documents/publications/dia­logue1_pcia_complete.pdf> (accessed 4 December 2010).

Homer-Dixon, T. F. (1994) 'Environmental Scarcities and Violent Conflict: Evidence from Cases', *International Security* 19 (1): 5–40.

Howell, J. (2006) 'The Global War on Terror, Development and Civil Society', *Journal of International Development* 18 (1): 121–35.

Human Security Report Project (2005) 'Human Security Report 2005: War and Peace in the Twenty-First Century', Human Security Centre, University of British Columbia, Vancouver and Oxford University Press, Oxford.

—— (2006) Human Security Brief 2006, Human Security Centre, University of British Columbia, Vancouver.

Huntington, S. P. (1968) *Political Order in Changing Societies*, Yale University Press, New Haven CT.

—— (1993) 'The Clash of Civilisations?' *Foreign Affairs* 72 (3): 22–50.

—— (1996) *The Clash of Civilisations and the Remaking of World Order*, Simon and Schuster, New York NY.

ICG (International Crisis Group) (2006) 'Resolving Timor-Leste's Crisis', Asia Report No. 120, October, Jakarta and Brussels.

—— (2008) 'Combating Sexual Violence in Conflict: Using Facts from the Ground', speech by Donald Steinberg to UN Action Against Sexual Violence in Conflict, December. <http://www.crisisgroup.org/en/publication-type/speeches/2008/combating-sexual-violence-in-conflict-using-facts-from-the-ground.aspx> (accessed 1 August 2010).

ICISS (2001), 'Responsibility to Protect', Report of the International Commission on Intervention and State Sovereignty, International Development Research Centre (IDRC), Ottawa.

ICRC (International Committee of the Red Cross) (2001) 'Women Facing War: ICRC Study on the Impact of Armed Conflict on Women', ICRC, Geneva. <http://www.icrc.org/Web/Eng/ site engo.nsf/htmlall/p0798/$File/ICRC=_002_0798_WOMEN_FACING_WAR.PDF> (accessed 27 July 2010).

IDMC (2010) 'Internal Displacement: a Global Overview of Trends and Developments in 2009', edited by N. M. Birkeland, K. Halff and E. Jennings, Internal Displacement Monitoring Centre, Geneva.

IDS (2010) 'An Upside Down View of Governance', Institute of Development Studies, University of Sussex.

International Alert (2002) 'Gender Mainstreaming in Peace Support Operations: Moving Beyond Rhetoric to Practice', report by D. Mazurana and E. P. Lopez, International Alert, London.

—— (2010) 'Programming Framework for International Alert: Design, Monitoring and Evaluation', International Alert, London. <http://www.internationalalert.org/about/files/Programming_Framework_2010.pdf> (accessed 15 December 2010).

International Dialogue on Peacebuilding and Statebuilding (2010) 'The Dili Declaration: a New Vision for Peacebuilding and Statebuilding'. <http://oecd.org/dataoecd/12/30/44927821.pdf> (accessed 6 March 2011).

Jabri, V. (1996) *Discourses on Violence: Conflict Analysis Reconsidered*, Manchester University Press, Manchester.

Jabri, V. and E. O' Gorman (eds) (1999) *Women, Culture and International Relations*, Lynne Rienner, Boulder CO and London.

Jackson, C. and R. Pearson (eds) (1998) *Feminist Visions of Development*, Routledge, London.

Jackson, R. and G. Sørensen (2010) *Introduction to International*

Relations: Theories and Approaches, fourth edition, Oxford University Press, Oxford.

Jacobs, S., R. Jacobson and J. Marchbank (2000) *States of Conflict: Gender, Violence and Resistance*, Zed Books, London.

Jacoby, T. (2008) *Understanding Conflict and Violence: Theoretical and Interdisciplinary Approaches*, Routledge, London.

Jeong, H. W. (2000) *Peace and Conflict Studies: an Introduction*, Ashgate, Aldershot.

—— (2008) *Understanding Conflict and Conflict Analysis*, Sage, London.

Kabeer, N. (1994) *Reversed Realities: Gender Hierarchies in Development Thought*, Verso, London.

Kaldor, M. (2006 [1999]) *New and Old Wars: Organised Violence in a Global Era*, second edition, Polity Press, Cambridge.

Kalyvas, S. (2001) '"New" and "Old" Civil Wars: a Valid Distinction?', *World Politics* 54 (1): 99–118.

Kant, I. (1939 [1795]) *Perpetual Peace* (Preface by N. Murray Butler), Columbia University Press, New York NY.

Kaplan, R. (1993) *Balkan Ghosts: a Journey Through History*, St Martin's Press, New York NY.

—— (1994) 'The Coming Anarchy: How Scarcity, Crime, Overpopulation and Disease are Rapidly Destroying the Social Fabric of our Planet', *Atlantic Monthly*, February. <http://www.theatlantic.com/magazine/archive/1994/02/the-coming-anarchy/4670/1/> (accessed 16 September 2010).

Kedourie, E. (1993 [1960]) *Nationalism*, fourth edition, Wiley-Blackwell, Oxford.

Keegan, J. (1993) *A History of Warfare*, Hutchinson, London.

Keen, D. (2005) *Conflict and Collusion in Sierra Leone*, James Currey, Oxford.

—— (2008) *Complex Emergencies*, Polity, Cambridge.

Kothari, U. (ed.) (2005a) *A Radical History of Development Studies: Institutions, Individuals, and Ideologies*, Zed Books, London.

—— (2005b) 'Authority and expertise: the professionalisation of international development and the ordering of dissent', *Antipode* 37 (3): 425–46.

Kriger, N. J. (1992) *Zimbabwe's Guerrilla War: Peasant Voices*, African

Studies Series, Cambridge University Press, Cambridge.

Le Billon, P. (2001) 'Angola's Political Economy of War: the Role of Oil and Diamonds, 1975–2000', *African Affairs* 100 (398): 55–80.

—— (2003) 'Buying Peace or Fuelling War: the Role of Corruption in Armed Conflict', *Journal of International Development* 15 (4): 413–26.

Leftwich, A. (2000) *States of Development: on the Primacy of Politics in Development*, Polity Press, Cambridge.

Leonhardt, M. (2003) 'Towards a Unified Methodology: Reframing PCIA' in A. Austin, M. Fischer and O. Wils (eds) *Peace and Conflict Impact Assessment: Critical Views on Theory and Practice* (Berghof Handbook Dialogue Series No. 1) Berghof Research Centre for Constructive Conflict Management, Berlin, pp. 53–66. <http://www.berghof-handbook.net/documents/publications/dialogue1_pcia_complete.pdf> (accessed 4 December 2010).

Lorenz, K. (1966) *On Aggression*, Meuthen, London.

Macrae, J. (2001) *Aiding Recovery? The Crisis of Aid in Chronic Political Emergencies*, Zed Books, London.

—— (2002) 'The New Humanitarianisms: a Review of Trends in Global Humanitarian Action' HPG Report No. 11, Humanitarian Policy Group, Overseas Development Institute, London.

Mack, A. (1975) 'Why Big Nations Lose Small Wars: The Politics of Asymmetric Conflict', *World Politics* 27 (2): 175–200.

Mack, R. and R. Snyder (1957) 'The analysis of social conflict – toward an overview and synthesis', *Journal of Conflict Resolution* 1 (4): 212–48.

Malešević, S. (2010) *The Sociology of War and Violence*, Cambridge University Press, Cambridge.

Mazo J. (2010) *Climate Conflict: How Global Warming Threatens Security and What to Do About It*, International Institute for Strategic Studies, London.

McLean Hilker, L. and E. Fraser (2009) 'Youth Exclusion, Violence, Conflict and Fragile States', report prepared for DFID's Equity and Rights Team, London. <http://www.gsdrc.org/docs/open/CON66.pdf> (accessed 6 December 2010).

Meintjes, S., M. Turshen and A. Pillay (2001) *The Aftermath: Women and Post-Conflict Transformation*, Zed Books, London.

Melander, E., M. Öberg et al. (2009) 'Are "New Wars" More Atrocious? Battle Intensity, Civilians Killed and Forced Migration before and after the End of the Cold War', *European Journal of International Relations* 15 (3): 505–36.

Menkhaus, K. (2004) *Somalia: State Collapse and Terrorism*, Adelphi Paper 364, Oxford University Press, Oxford.

Miller, N. E. (1965) 'The Frustration-Aggression Hypothesis' in P. R. Lawson (ed.), *Frustration: the Development of a Scientific Concept*, Macmillan, New York NY.

Mitchell, C. R. (1981) *The Structure of International Conflict*, Macmillan, London.

Mohanty, C. (1988) 'Under Western Eyes: Feminist Scholarship and Colonial Discourses' *Feminist Review* 30 (Autumn): 61–88.

—— (1995) 'Feminist Encounters: Locating the Politics of Experience' in L. Nicholson and S. Seidman (eds), *Social Postmodernism: Beyond Identity Politics*, Cambridge University Press, Cambridge.

Molyneux, M. (1985) 'Mobilisation without Emancipation? Women's Interests, State and Revolution in Nicaragua', *Feminist Studies* 11 (2): 227–54.

Moore, J. (ed.) (1998) *Hard Choices: Moral Dilemmas in Humanitarian Intervention*, Rowman and Littlefield, Lanham MD.

Moser, C. O. N. (1991) 'Gender Planning in the Third World: Meeting Practical and Strategic Needs' in R. Grant and K. Newland (eds), *Gender and International Relations*, Open University Press, Buckingham, pp. 83–121.

—— (1993) *Gender Planning and Development: Theory, Practice and Training*, Routledge, London.

Moser, C. O. N. and F. C. Clarke (eds) (2001) *Victims, Perpetrators or Actors? Gender, Armed Conflict and Political Violence*, Zed Books, London.

Myrttinen, H. (2003) 'Disarming Masculinities', *Disarmament Forum* 4 (Special Issue on Women, Men, Peace and Security), United Nations Institute for Disarmament Research (UNIDIR), Geneva.

—— (2008) 'Sketching the Militias: Constructions of Violent Masculinity in the East Timor Conflict' in D. Zarkov (ed.), *Gender, Violent Conflict and Development*, Zubaan, New Delhi, pp. 180–201.

Naraghi-Anderlini, S. (2007) *Women Building Peace: What They Do, Why It Matters*, Lynne Rienner, Boulder CO and London.

—— (2001) 'Women, Peace and Security: a Policy Audit, From Beijing Platform for Action to UN Security Council Resolution 1325', report commissioned by International Alert, London.

Nardin, T. (1980) 'Theory and practice in conflict research' in T. R. Gurr (ed.), *Handbook of Political Conflict: Theory and Research*, The Free Press, New York NY.

Newman, E. (2004) 'The "New Wars" Debate: a Historical Perspective Is Needed', *Security Dialogue* 35 (2): 173–89.

NORAD (2007), 'Review of Development Cooperation in Timor-Leste', report, Embassy of Norway (Jakarta) and NORAD.

Nordstrom, C. (1997) *A Different Kind of War Story*, University of Pennsylvania Press, Philadelphia PA.

—— (2004) *Shadows of War: Violence, Power and International Profiteering in the Twenty-First Century*, University of California Press, Berkeley CA.

—— (2007) *Global Outlaws: Crime, Money and Power in the Contemporary World*, University of California Press, Berkeley CA.

Nyheim, D. (2008) 'Can Violence, War and State Collapse Be Prevented? The Future of Operational Conflict Early Warning and Response Systems', discussion paper commissioned by the OECD DAC International Network on Conflict and Fragility, Paris. <http://www.carleton.ca/cifp/app/serve.php/1158.pdf> (accessed 15 December 2010).

O'Connell, H. (ed.) (1993) 'Women and Conflict', *Oxfam Focus on Gender* 1 (2).

Obermayer, Z., C. J. L. Murray and E. Gakidou (2008) 'Fifty Years of Violent War Deaths from Vietnam to Bosnia: Analysis of Data from the World Health Survey Programme', *British Medical Journal* 336 (7659): 1482–6A.

OECD (2000) 'Guidelines for Multinational Enterprises', OECD, Paris. <http://www.oecd.org/about/0,3347,en_2649_34889_1_1_1_1_1,00.html> (accessed 10 October 2010).

—— (2007) 'Encouraging Effective Evaluation of Conflict Prevention and Peacebuilding Activities: Towards DAC Guidance', offprint of *OECD Journal on Development* 8 (3): 3–102, authored by M. B.

Anderson, D. Chigas and P. Woodrow. <http://www.oecd.org/dataoecd/52/3/39660852.pdf> (accessed 10 March 2011).

—— (2009) 'Armed Violence Reduction: Enabling Development', Policy Paper prepared by INCAF, OECD, Paris.

OECD DAC (1998) 'Conflict, Peace and Development Cooperation on the Threshold of the Twenty-First Century', DAC Development Cooperation Guideline Series, OECD, Paris.

—— (2001) 'The DAC Guidelines: Helping to Prevent Violent Conflict' (includes the original 1997 report 'Conflict, Peace and Development Cooperation on the Threshold of the Twenty-First Century'), OECD, Paris. <http://www.oecd.org/dataoecd/15/54/1886146.pdf> (accessed 6 December 2010).

—— (2004) 'Security System Reform and Governance', DAC Guidelines and Reference Series, OECD, Paris. <www.oecd.org/dataoecd/8/39/31785288.pdf> (accessed 10 March 2011).

—— (2007) 'Principles for Good International Engagement in Fragile States and Situations', OECD, Paris.

—— (2008) 'Concepts and Dilemmas of State Building in Fragile Situations: from Fragility to Resilience', OECD DAC discussion paper, offprint of OECD *Journal on Development* 9 (3): 5–79 (authored by B. Jones, R. Chandran, E. Cousens, J. Slotin and J. Sherman), OECD, Paris.

—— (2009a) 'Official development assistance over fifty years', OECD, Paris. <http://www.oecd.org/document/41/0,3343,en_2649_34447_46195625_1_1_1_1,00.html> (accessed 2 November 2010).

—— (2010a) 'Ensuring Fragile States Are Not Left Behind', summary report, International Network on Conflict and Fragility, OECD, Paris.

—— (2010b) 'Development aid rose in 2009 and most donors will meet 2010 targets', OECD, Paris. <http://www.oecd.org/document/11/0,3343,en_2649_34447_44981579_1_1_1_1,00.html> (accessed 2 November 2010).

O' Gorman, E. (1999) 'Writing Women's Wars: Foucauldian Strategies of Engagement', in V. Jabri and E. O' Gorman (eds), *Women, Culture and International Relations*, Lynne Rienner, Boulder CO.

Oxfam IANSA and Saferworld (2007) 'Africa's Missing Billions:

International Arms Flows and the Cost of Conflict', Oxfam, Oxford.

PAC (Partnership Africa Canada) (2000) 'The Heart of the Matter: Sierra Leone, Diamonds and Human Security', PAC report, Ottawa.

Paris, R. (2002) 'International Peacebuilding and the 'Mission Civilisatrice', *Review of International Studies* 28 (4): 637–56.

—— (2004) *At War's End: Building Peace after Civil Conflict*, Cambridge University Press, Cambridge.

—— (2006) 'Bringing the Leviathan Back in: Classical Versus Contemporary Studies of the Liberal Peace', *International Studies Review* 8 (3): 425–40.

—— (2010) 'Saving Liberal Peacebuilding', *Review of International Studies* 36 (2): 337–65.

Paris, R. and T. D. Sisk (eds) (2009) *The Dilemmas of Statebuilding: Confronting the Contradiction of Postwar Peace Operations*, Routledge, New York NY.

Parpart, J. L. and M. Zalewski (2008) *Rethinking the Man Question: Sex, Gender and Violence in International Relations*, Zed Books, London.

Peterson, V. S. (ed.) (1992) *Gendered States: Feminist (Re)Visions of International Relations Theory*, Lynne Rienner, Boulder CO.

Peterson, V. S. and A. S. Runyan (1993) *Global Gender Issues*, Westview Press, Boulder CO.

Pettman, J. J. (1996) *Worlding Women: a Feminist International Politics*, Routledge, London and New York NY.

Polman, L. (2010) *War Games: the Story of Aid and War in Modern Times*, Penguin, London.

Pouligny, B. (2006) *Peace Operations Seen from Below: UN Missions and Local People*, Hurst and Company, London.

Pugh, M. (2005) 'The Political Economy of Peacebuilding: a Critical Theory Perspective', *International Journal of Peace Studies* 10 (2): 23–42.

Ramsbotham, O. and T. Woodhouse (1996) *Humanitarian Intervention in Contemporary Conflict: a Reconceptualisation*. Polity Press, Cambridge.

Ramsbotham, O., T. Woodhouse and H. Miall (2005) *Contemporary Conflict Resolution*, second edition, Polity Press, Cambridge.

Rehn, E. and E. Johnson Sirleaf (2002), 'Women, War and Peace: the

Independent Experts' Assessment on the Impact of Armed Conflict on Women and Women's Role in Peace-Building', UNIFEM, New York NY. <http://www.unifem.org/materials/item_detail.php?productID=17> (accessed 1 August 2010).

Richards, P. (ed.) (1996) *Fighting for the Rainforest: War, Youth and Resources in Sierra Leone*, James Currey, Oxford.

—— (2005) *No Peace No War: an Anthropology of Contemporary Armed Conflict*, Ohio University Press, Athens and James Currey, Oxford.

Richmond, O. P. (2008a) *Peace in International Relations*, Routledge, London.

—— (2008b) 'Reclaiming Peace in International Relations', *Millennium* 36 (3): 439–70.

Richmond, O. P. and R. MacGinty (eds) (2007) 'The Liberal Peace and Post-Conflict Reconstruction', *Global Society* 21 (3) (special issue).

Richmond, O. P. and J. Franks (eds) (2009) *Liberal Peace Transitions: between Statebuilding and Peacebuilding*, Edinburgh University Press, Edinburgh.

Ridd, R. and E. Callaway (1986) (eds) *Caught Up in Conflict: Women's Responses to Political Strife*, Macmillan, London.

Riddell, R. G. (2007) *Does Foreign Aid Really Work?* Oxford University Press, Oxford.

Rist, G. (2008) *The History of Development: from Western Origins to Global Faith*, third edition, Zed Books, London.

Roberts, A. (2010) 'Lives and Statistics: Are 90 Per Cent of War Victims Civilians?' *Survival* 52 (3): 115–36.

Rogers, P. and O. Ramsbotham (1999) 'Then and Now: Peace Research – Past and Future', *Political Studies* 47 (4): 740–54.

Runge, P. (2009) 'The Provincial Reconstruction Teams in Afghanistan: Role Model for Civil–Military Relations?', Occasional Paper 4, Bonn International Centre for Conversion (BICC), Bonn.

Saferworld (2009) 'Climate Change and Conflict: Lessons from Community Conservancies in Northern Kenya', Conservation Development Centre (CDC), the International Institute for Sustainable Development (IISD) and Saferworld, Nairobi. <http://www.saferworld.org.uk/downloads/pubdocs/Climate%20change%20and%20

conflict.pdf> (accessed 14 October 2010).

Scott, J. C. (1977) 'Peasant Revolution: a Dismal Science', review article, *Comparative Politics* 9 (3): 231–48.

Shawcross, W. (2000) *Deliver Us from Evil: Warlords and Peacekeepers in a World of Endless Conflict*, Bloomsbury, London.

Shearer (2001) 'Aiding of Abetting? Humanitarian Aid and its Economic Role in Civil War' in M. Berdal and D. M. Malone (eds), *Greed and Grievance: Economic Agendas in Civil Wars*, Lynne Rienner, Boulder CO, pp. 189–204.

Shepherd, L. J. (2008) *Gender, Violence and Security: Discourse as Practice*. Zed Books, London.

—— (ed.) (2010) *Gender Matters in Global Politics: a Feminist Introduction to International Relations*, Routledge, London.

Sherriff, A. with K. Barnes (2008) 'Study for the Slovenian Presidency on Enhancing the EU Response to Women and Armed Conflict', European Centre for Development Policy Management, Maastricht.

SIDA (2006) 'Manual for Conflict Analysis', Swedish International Development Assistance, Stockholm. <http://www.conflictsensitivity.org/sites/default/files/Manual_for_Conflict_Analysis.pdf> (accessed 10 March 2011).

SIPRI (Stockholm International Peace Research Institute) (2009) *SIPRI Yearbook 2009: Armaments, Disarmament and International Security*, Oxford University Press, Oxford.

—— (2010) *SIPRI Yearbook 2010: Armaments, Disarmament and International Security*, Oxford University Press, Oxford.

Sisk, T. D. (2008) 'Peacebuilding as Democratization: Findings and Recommendations' in A. K. Jarstad and T. D. Sisk (eds), *From War to Democracy: Dilemmas of Peacebuilding*, Cambridge University Press, Cambridge.

Sjoberg, L. and C. E. Gentry (2007) *Mothers, Monsters, Whores: Women's Violence in Global Politics*, Zed Books, London.

Slim, H. (2001) 'Violence and Humanitarianism: Moral Paradox and the Protection of Civilians', *Security Dialogue* 32 (3): 325–39.

Smith, A. D. (1991) *National Identity*, Penguin, London.

—— (1993) 'The Ethnic Sources of Nationalism', *Survival: Global Politics and Strategy* 35 (1): 48–62.

Smith, D. and J. Vivekananda (2009) 'Climate Change, Conflict and

Fragility: Understanding the Linkages, Shaping Effective Responses', International Alert and European Commission, London and Brussels. <http://www.international-alert.org/press/Climate_change_conflict_and_fragility_Nov09.pdf> (accessed 13 October 2010).

Spagat, M., A. Mack, T. Cooper and J. Kreutz (2009) 'Estimating War Deaths: an Arena of Contestation', *Journal of Conflict Resolution* 53 (6): 934–50.

Specht, I. (2006) 'Red Shoes: Experiences of Girl-Combatants in Liberia', report, International Labour Organisation, Geneva. <http://www.transitioninternational.com/?Portfolio_and_Services:Recent_Publications> (accessed 30 July 2010).

Stepanova, E. (2008) *Terrorism in Asymmetrical Conflict: Ideological and Structural Aspects*, SIPRI Research Report No. 23, Oxford University Press, Oxford.

Stewart, F. (2003) 'Horizontal Inequalities: a Neglected Dimension of Development', CRISE Working Paper 1, Centre for Research on Inequality, Human Security and Ethnicity, University of Oxford.

—— (ed.) (2008) *Horizontal Inequalities and Conflict: Understanding Group Violence in Multiethnic Societies*, Palgrave Macmillan, London.

Stewart, F., V. Fitzgerald et al. (2001) *War and Underdevelopment: the Economic and Social Consequences of Conflict*, Volume 1, Oxford University Press, Oxford.

Suhrke, A. (2001) 'Peacekeepers and Nation-builders: Dilemmas of the UN in East Timor', *International Peacekeeping* 8 (4): 1–20.

Sylvester, C. (1987) 'Some Dangers in Merging Feminist and Peace Projects', *Alternatives* 12 (4): 493–509.

—— (1994) *Feminist Theory and International Relations*, Cambridge University Press, Cambridge.

Tickner, J. A. (1992) *Gender in International Relations: Feminist Perspectives on Achieving Global Security*, Columbia University Press, New York NY.

—— (2001) *Gendering World Politics: Issues and Approaches in the Post-Cold War Era*, Columbia University Press, New York NY.

Tilly, C. (ed.) (1975) *The Formation of National States in Western Europe*, Princeton University Press, Princeton NJ.

UN (1995) 'Supplement to Agenda for Peace: Position Paper of the Secretary-General on the Occasion of the Fiftieth Anniversary of the United Nations', A/50/60– S/1995/1, United Nations, New York NY.

—— (2000) 'Report of the Panel on United Nations Peace Operations', A/55/305–S/2000/809, United Nations, New York, NY.

—— (2001) 'Report of the Secretary-General on Prevention of Armed Conflict', A/55/985–S/2001/574, United Nations, New York, NY.

—— (2002) 'Women, Peace and Security: a Study Submitted by the Secretary-General Pursuant to Security Council Resolution 1325 (2000)', United Nations, New York NY.

—— (2003) 'Report of the Panel of Experts on the Illegal Exploitation of Natural Resources and Other Forms of Wealth of the Democratic Republic of Congo', Report to the Security Council, S/2003/1027, New York NY, October.

—— (2004) 'A More Secure World: Our Shared Responsibility', Report of the Secretary-General's High-Level Panel on Threats, Challenges and Change, A/59/565, United Nations, New York NY.

—— (2005) 'In Larger Freedom: Towards Security, Development and Human Rights for All', Report of the Secretary-General to the Security Council, A/59/2005, United Nations, New York NY.

—— (2006a) Report of the United Nations Independent Special Commission of Inquiry for Timor-Leste, Geneva, October.

—— (2006b) Report of the Secretary-General on Timor-Leste Pursuant to Security Council Resolution 1690 (2006), S/2006/628, August.

—— (2008) 'Protect, Respect and Remedy: a Framework for Business and Human Rights', Report of the Special Representative of the Secretary-General on human rights and transnational corporations and other business enterprises, A/HRC/8/5, Geneva, 7 April.

—— (2009a) 'Report of Secretary-General pursuant to Security Council resolution 1820 (2008)', S/2009/362, United Nations, New York NY.

—— (2009b) 'Report of the Group of Experts on the Democratic Republic of Congo', Report to the Security Council, S/2009/603, United Nations, New York NY, November.

—— (2009c) 'Implementing the Responsibility to Protect', Report of the Secretary-General to the 63rd session of the General Assembly,

A/63/677, follow-up to the outcome of the Millennium Summit, United Nations, New York NY.

—— (2010a) 'Review of the United Nations Peacebuilding Architecture', S/2010/393, United Nations, New York NY.

—— (2010b) 'Report of the Secretary-General on the implementation of Security Council resolutions 1820 (2008) and 1888 (2009)', S/2010/604, United Nations, New York NY.

UNDP (1994) *Human Development Report 1994: New Dimensions of Human Security*, UNDP and Oxford University Press, New York NY and Oxford.

—— (2000) 'The Role of UNDP in Crisis and Post-Conflict Situations', Executive Board Paper, DP/2001/4, UNDP, New York NY. <http://www.undp.org/execbrd/pdf/dp01-4.PDF> (accessed 2 November 2010).

—— (2002) 'Human Development Report 2002: Quotable Facts'. <http://hdr.undp.org/en/media/HDR_2002_Facts.pdf> (accessed 27 October 2010).

—— (2003) 'Conflict-Related Development Analysis', Bureau for Crisis Prevention and Recovery, New York NY. <http://www.undp.org/cpr/documents/prevention/integrate/CDA_complete.pdf> (accessed 10 March 2011).

—— (2005) *Human Development Report 2005. International Cooperation at a Crossroads: Aid, Trade and Security in an Unequal World*, Oxford University Press, Oxford.

—— (2009) *Human Development Report 2009. Overcoming barriers: Human mobility and development*, United Nations, New York NY.

UN DPKO (2005) 'Gender and UN Peacekeeping Operations', UN Department of Peacekeeping Operations, New York NY. <http://www.un.org/en/peacekeeping/publications/gender_brochure.pdf> (accessed 10 July 2010).

—— (2010) 'UN Peacekeeping Factsheet', Department of Peacekeeping Operations, New York NY. <http://www.un.org/en/peacekeeping/documents/factsheet.pdf> (accessed 28 October 2010).

UN Millennium Project (2005) 'Investing in Development: a Practical Plan to Achieve the Millennium Goals', UN, New York NY.

UN Security Council (1999) Resolution 1272, S/RES/1272 (1999), New York NY, 25 October.

—— (2000) Resolution 1325, S/RES/1325 (2000), New York NY, 31 October.

—— (2008a) Resolution 1820, S/RES/1820 (2008), New York NY, 19 June.

—— (2008b) 'Fourth Special Report of the Secretary-General on the United Nations Organization Mission in the Democratic Republic of Congo, November 2008', S/2008/728, para. 47.

USAID (2004) 'Conducting a Conflict Assessment: a Framework for Strategy and Program Development', US Agency for International Development, Washington DC. <http://www.usaid.gov/our_work/cross-cutting_programs/conflict/publications/docs/CMM_ConflAssessFrmwrk_8-17-04.pdf> (accessed 14 October).

Uvin, P. (1998) *Aiding Violence: the Development Enterprise in Rwanda*, Kumarian Press, Bloomfield CT.

Walker, B. (ed.) (1994) 'Women and Emergencies', Oxfam Focus on Gender 4, Oxfam, Oxford.

Webb, K. (1986) 'Conflict: Inherent and Contingent Theories', *World Encyclopedia of Peace*, Vol. 1, Pergamon Press, Oxford, pp. 169–74.

—— (1992) 'Science, Biology and Conflict', *Paradigms* 6: 65–96.

Weiss, T. G. (2007) *Humanitarian Intervention: Ideas in Action*, Polity Press, Cambridge.

Wheeler, N. J. (2002) *Saving Strangers: Humanitarian Intervention in International Society*. Oxford University Press, Oxford.

Williams, A. (2006) 'Reconstruction: the Bringing of Peace and Plenty or Occult Imperialism?', *Global Society* 21 (3): 539–51.

Williams, P. D. (ed.) (2008) *Security Studies: an Introduction*, Routledge, London.

Wilson, E. O. (1975) *Sociobiology: the New Synthesis*, Harvard University Press, Cambridge MA.

Woodward, S. L. (2001) 'Humanitarian War: a New Consensus?', *Disasters* 25 (4): 331–4.

World Bank (2003) *Breaking the Conflict Trap: Civil War and Development Policy*, World Bank and Oxford University Press, Oxford.

—— (2007) 'Timor-Leste's Youth in Crisis: Situation Analysis and Policy Options', World Bank, Washington DC. <http://siteresources.world-

bank.org/INTTIMORLESTE/Resources/youngincrisienglish.pdf> (accessed 6 December 2010).

—— (2010) 'Violence in the City: Understanding and Supporting Community Responses to Urban Violence', Social Development Department, Conflict, Crime and Violence Team, World Bank, Washington DC.

Wrong, M. (2009) *'It's Our Turn to East': the Story of a Kenyan Whistle-blower*, Fourth Estate, London.

Yanacopulos, H. and J. Hanlon (eds) (2006) *Civil War, Civil Peace*, Open University and James Currey, Milton Keynes and Oxford.

Zarkov, D. (ed.) (2008) *Gender, Violent Conflict and Development*, Lynne Rienner, Boulder, CO.

Zartman, William I. (1995) 'Introduction: Posing the Problem of State Collapse', in William I. Zartman (ed.) *Collapsed States: The Disintegration and Restoration of Legitimate Authority*, Lynne Rienner, Boulder, CO.

Zimmerman, E. (1983) *Political Violence, Crises and Revolutions*, Schenkman, Rochester, VT.

Index

9/11 30, 68, 77, 128

Abbas, Mahmoud 49
Abirafeh, Lina 112
academic approaches to conflict
   and development 10-13
accountability 18, 75, 78, 84,
   109, 121, 133
Afghanistan 4, 5, 8, 9, 19, 40, 41,
   49, 87, 91, 107, 111-12, 114,
   121, 128-31
Africa Peace and Security
   Architecture (APSA) 88
Africa Peace Forum in Kenya
   (APFO) 51
African Centre for Constructive
   Resolution of Disputes
   (ACCORD) 88
African Union (AU) 86, 88
agency 20-1, 29, 36, 43, 47, 92,
   93, 97-8, 111-13, 117-19; *see
   also* participation
Agency for Cooperation and
   Research in Development
   (ACORD) 106
aggression 20, 22-3, 27-30
aid, coding of 90; compromised
   in conflict situations 3, 134;
   cost of 123-4; critical views of
   10, 17-18, 124, 127, 133-4;

fuels conflict 37, 124; and
   humanitarianism 18; levels of
   9; and liberal principles 7;
   and politics and peacebuilding
   15-17, 66-91; securitisation of
   18-19, 116, 133-4
Al-Ali, Nadje 111
Albania 69
Algeria 8
Al-Qaida 8
'An Agenda for Peace' 1, 3, 64,
   74, 132
Anderson, Benedict 26
Anderson, Mary 14, 50
Angola 4, 32-3, 34
Annan, Kofi 68
anti-Semitism 30
arms trade and proliferation 3, 5,
   34-7, 43, 56, 66, 68-9, 72, 81,
   82-3 (*box*), 90
asymmetric warfare 135, 170n
Australia 85, 122, 123
Austria 40
Azerbaijan 131

Beall, J. 116, 130
Bellamy, A. J. 71
Berdal, Matt 127
Boserup, Ester 93
Bosnia and Herzegovina 4, 25,

30, 73, 98
Boutros-Ghali, Boutros 1, 3
Bradbury, Mark 126-7
Brahimi Report 73
Brownmiller, Susan 96
Burguieres, Mary 95
Burkina Faso 41
Burundi 39, 41, 76, 85, 87
Bush, George W. 31
Bush, Kenneth 44, 50, 64, 132

Cambodia 4, 74, 85, 118
Canada 70
capacity building 47, 70, 78, 79-
    80, 88, 90, 122-3, 124
Carnegie Commission for
    Preventing Deadly Conflict
    (1997) 72
caste system 21
Central African Republic 6, 8, 40,
    41, 76
Centre for Conflict Resolution in
    Uganda (CECORE) 51
Centre for Humanitarian
    Dialogue (CHD) 88
Chad 40, 41
Chechnya 98
child soldiers 6, 43, 90, 101, 108
China 123
Christianity 26, 31
civil society 10, 35, 55, 60, 72,
    77, 81, 84, 88, 94, 105, 117-
    18, 127, 128, 135
civil wars 3, 4, 31-2, 47
civilians, armed 1; as victims and
    targets 1, 6, 163n; and peace-
    building 4; and security sector
    reform 84
'clash of civilisations' 26-7, 39
climate change 84-6 (box 85)

Cold War 1, 3, 5, 6, 7, 25, 30,
    87, 91, 136, 161n
Collaborative for Development
    Action (Boston) 50, 52
Collier, Paul 31-3, 36
Colombia 6, 9, 41
colonial legacies 42, 95, 101-2,
    119, 121-3
community-based organisations
    16, 74, 77
conflict analysis frameworks 22-
    3, 44-65 (box 51-2)
conflict analysis matrix 54-6
conflict attitudes 31, 47
conflict behaviour 46-7
conflict diamonds (box) 34-5
conflict management 12, 20, 39,
    87, 134
conflict prevention 4, 15, 16, 29,
    45, 48, 59, 67, 69, 72-3, 75,
    86, 89, 90, 116, 130, 132
conflict reduction 13, 15, 57, 63
conflict resolution 12, 15, 63, 64,
    65, 68, 80, 90, 130, 131
conflict sensitivity 15-16, 45, 49-
    52, 58-62
conflict transformation 2, 12, 42,
    45, 64, 95-105, 113, 131-2,
    134, 135
conflict, actors in 53; causes and
    drivers 52; and change 15, 22,
    24; cycles or stages of 48-9;
    and development programmes
    80-4; 'dividers and connectors'
    in 53; dynamics and events in
    53; ethnic 4, 25-6, 33, 42; and
    evolution theory 22-3; indirect
    and direct conflict program-
    ming 57-8; and inequality 15,
    22, 24, 33, 38-9, 52, 72, 75;

inherent or contingent? 20, 22, 25-30, 42; levels of analysis 47; objectivist and subjectivist explanations 20-1, 24, 31, 36, 42-3; origins of the development–conflict relationship 13-19; political economy explanations 21; politics of analysing 20-43; and poverty 3, 15, 20-43 (*box* 40-1), 50, 67, 69, 72, 75, 77; regional 47, 68; and relative deprivation 20, 27-31, 38, 42; and religion 26; scenarios of 53; structural 20-1, 22, 23-4, 42, 52; three key debates (*box*) 20-1; as triad (*diagram*) 46; triggers of 53; working in, on, or around 16

Connell, Rob (Raewyn) 102

Consortium of Humanitarian Agencies in Sri Lanka (CHA) 51

corporate responsibility 35

corruption 17-18, 34, 37, 55, 78, 135

Côte d'Ivoire 8, 35, 106

counter-insurgency 5-6, 13, 112, 129-30, 134

counter-terrorism 116, 134, 135

Cramer, Chris 36, 39

crime, organised 4, 6, 32, 37, 68-9, 77, 83, 134

Curle, Adam 24

Darfur 71, 86, 87, 88, 107

Darwin, Charles 22

de Mello, Sergio Vieira 121

de Waal, Alex 127-8

Democratic Republic of Congo 6, 8, 9, 33, 34, 40, 41, 84, 85,

87, 104, 107, 110, 113, 121

democratisation 7, 10, 33, 64, 72, 75

Department for International Development (DFID) (UK) 50, 51, 52, 54, 63, 79-80, 87, 88, 133

development and peacebuilding 3-10, 44, 48, 62, 64, 65, 66-91 (esp. 73-7), 86, 90-1, 94, 99, 101, 103, 112, 113; 115-36

diamonds *see* conflict diamonds, natural resources

diasporas 32

Dili Declaration 78

diplomacy 3, 4, 15-16, 49, 71, 72-3. 79, 90, 115, 127, 129, 132

disarmament, demobilisation and reintegration (DDR) programmes 16, 55, 58, 68, 74, 81, 82, 90, 101, 105, 108-9, 125, 127

'do no harm' 14, 15, 16, 39, 44, 52, 53, 61, 63, 64, 78, 134

Doyle, Michael 7

drugs 6, 37, 83

Duffield, Mark 5, 68, 116

Dunant, Henri 16–17

Economic Community of West African States (ECOWAS) 47, 82

economic essentialism 31-7

education 14, 31, 32, 41, 46, 55, 57, 72, 124, 128

Egypt 85

El Salvador 4, 117-18

elections 4, 49, 53, 56, 74, 76, 81, 123, 124, 125, 126

Elshtain, Jean Bethke 97
employment 59-60, 81
Enloe, Cynthia 95-7, 100, 113
environmental degradation 3, 12, 21, 35, 69, 84-6
Ethiopia 8, 85, 130
ethnic cleansing 25, 70
ethnic conflict 4, 25-6, 33, 42
European Peacebuilding Liaison Office 88
European Security Strategy 68
European Union (EU) 54, 62, 68, 87, 88, 106
evaluation 57, 58, 62, 63, 73; *see also* monitoring
exclusion 78, 80
exit points 119

facts and figures on development and conflict (*box*) 8-9
failed and fragile states 1, 5, 18, 40, 68, 77-80, 89, 91, 115-36, 167n
Failed States Index (FSI) 40
female-headed households 55
feminist International Relations 93-4, 101
Feyen, C. 64
Fiji 41
Fisher, Simon 132
Forum on EarlyWarning and Early Response (FEWER) 51
Franks, J. 133
Freud, Sigmund 27
frustration/aggression hypothesis 20, 27-9

Galtung, Johan 23-4, 40, 45, 64, 80, 165n
Gaza 49, 130

gender, and aggression 23; and DDR in Liberia 108-9 (*box*); and equality 23; Gender and Development (research focus) 93, 101; gendering of conflict and development 92-114; mainstreaming of 94, 106; protection 74; and role-playing 95-8; and transformation 98-105, 113
genocide 25, 69, 70, 71, 128
Gentry, Caroline 97-8
Georgia 40, 87
Germany 85
Ghana 35
Giddens, Anthony 43
Gleneagles G8 Summit (2005) 17
Global Peace Index 40-1
Global South 10, 42, 134
Global Witness 34-5
globalisation 4, 5, 10, 25, 42, 127
Goodfellow, T. 116
Goodhand, Jonathan 50
governance 1, 6, 15-16, 18, 19, 47, 50, 62, 63, 69, 77, 81, 83-4, 85, 119-28, 129, 133-4
Governance and Social Development Resource Centre (GSDRC) 52
Grindle, M. 126
group dynamics 30-1
Gsänger, H. 64
GTZ 51, 54
Guinea 40
Guinea-Bissau 41, 76
Gurr, Ted 29

Haiti 118
Hamas 49
health 14, 41, 67, 128

HIV/Aids 3, 69
Hobbes, Thomas 23
Hoeffler, Anke 31-3, 36
Howell, J. 129-30
Human Development Index
    (HDI) 41, 67
Human Development Report
    (HDR) 41, 67
human rights 3, 4, 7, 35, 40, 62,
    68, 69, 71, 72, 74, 75, 80, 81,
    93, 118, 122, 128
humanitarian intervention 1, 3-5,
    68, 69-71, 72, 128-9, 166n,
    167n
Huntington, Samuel P. 26-7, 39

Iceland 40
identity politics, 10, 23, 25-7, 38,
    94, 95, 97, 100, 105, 112-13,
    120
indirect and direct conflict pro-
    grammes 57-8
Indonesia 41, 122
informal economy 39
Institute of Development Studies
    (IDS) 105-6
internally displaced persons
    (IDPs) 1, 9, 40, 55, 81
International Alert 50, 51, 88,
    106
International Committee of the
    Red Cross (ICRC) 17, 106,
    129
International Conflict and
    Fragility network (INCAF) 89
International Crisis Group (ICG)
    62-3, 88
International Labour
    Organisation (ILO) 59-60
Interpeace 88

intra-state wars 5-6, 8, 69
Iraq 4, 5, 8, 9, 19, 40, 41, 49, 87,
    91, 111, 114, 121, 128-31
Islam 26, 31, 112
Israel 40, 46, 49

Jabri, Vivienne 43
Jacoby, T. 44
Japan 40, 123
Johnson-Sirleaf, Ellen 103

Kabeer, Naila 99
Kaldor, Mary 5
Kant, Immanuel 7, 161n
Kenya 85
Kimberley process 34
Kosovo 4, 69, 74, 87, 92, 121
Kothari, Uma 119

land 42, 46, 49, 52, 55
landmines 3, 56, 66, 81
Lao PDR 85
Lebanon 41
Leonhardt, Manuela 65
liberal peace 3-10, 39, 68, 71,
    115-16, 119, 121, 127-8, 161n
Liberia 9, 25, 48, 101, 103, 106,
    107, 108-9
local perceptions and participa-
    tion 56, 57-8, 61, 64, 68, 77,
    80, 83, 86, 115, 117-19, 120,
    123, 125, 127, 129-30, 134
Lord's Resistance Army 6
Lorenz, Konrad 23

Macedonia 74
Make Poverty History campaign
    17
Malešević, Siniša 43
Mali 41

Marxism 11, 24
media 25, 31, 72, 98
migration 54, 59-60, 108, 134
militarisation 52, 53, 55, 77, 94,
   95-7, 100-2, 110, 112-13
Millennium Development Goals
   (MDGs) 9, 13-14, 83, 164n
Mitchell, Chris 45-6
Mohanty, Chandra 102
Molyneux, Maxine 98-100
monitoring 4, 35, 57, 61, 63, 73;
   see also evaluation
Moser, Caroline 99
Mozambique 4, 101
Myanmar 41
Myrttinen, Henri 105

Namibia 4
nation building 74, 120-1, 123
nationalism 4, 25, 26, 100, 120
natural resource conflicts (especially minerals) 3, 4, 6, 32-7,
   43, 46, 52, 55, 72, 86, 110,
   122
neo-conservatives 31
neo-liberalism 10, 25, 42, 64,
   117, 119, 121, 134-5
Nepal 9, 41
Netanyahu, Binyamin 49
new wars 3-10, 39, 42
New Zealand 40
Nicaragua 98, 101
Niger 41
Nigeria 8
Nightingale, Florence 16-17
non-governmental organisations
   (NGOs), and gender 106; and
   local ownership/engagement
   117; and national identity 130;
   and neo-liberal order 10; and

conflict analysis 50, 54, 60;
   and conflict awareness 14, 16;
   and conflict sensitivity 51; and
   'Nightingale risk' 16-17; 64,
   66; proliferation of 88, 135;
   tensions within 90-1; women's
   92
Nordstrom, Carolyn 43
North Atlantic Treaty
   Organisation (NATO) 70, 87
Northern Ireland 30, 39
Norway 40, 85, 124; NORAD
   124

Occupied Territories 41
Organisation for Economic Co-
   operation and Development,
   Development Assistance
   Committee (OECD DAC), and
   coding of aid 90; forum 89-90;
   Guidelines (2001) 74-5, 89; on
   fragile states 78, 79, 89-90; on
   gender and conflict 106;
   International Conflict and
   Fragility network (INCAF) 89;
   Network on Conflict
   Prevention and Development
   87, 89; and security sector
   reform 84, 89
Oxfam 105

Pakistan 8, 40, 41
Palestine 46, 49, 92, 94, 130
Palestine Liberation Organisation
   (PLO) 49
Palestinian Authority 49
Paris, R. 125-6
participation 7, 18, 36, 54, 60,
   61, 64, 75, 96-8, 100, 103,
   107, 117-19; *see also* agency

Partnership Africa Canada 34-5
peace and conflict impact assessment (PCIA) 50, 56, 58-65, 132
peace, negative and positive 24, 40, 64, 67, 80, 133, 134
peacebuilding and development 3-10, 44, 48, 62, 64, 65, 66-91 (esp. 73–7), 86, 90-1, 94, 99, 101, 103, 112, 113; 115-36
Peacebuilding Fund 76
peacekeeping 3, 4, 9, 14, 40, 48, 69, 72, 73-4, 86, 87, 88, 90, 103, 107, 109, 110, 112, 122, 123, 130, 162n, 169n
peacemaking 3, 45, 48, 50, 69, 88, 103, 107, 132
Pettman, Jan Jindy 92, 97, 100, 102
policing 4, 66, 84, 90, 122, 124-5
policy formulation on development and conflict 22, 33, 44, 66-91
Portugal 122, 123, 124
post-structuralism 12
Pouligni, Béatrice 117-118
poverty, and conflict 37-43, 50, 67, 69, 72, 75, 77, 80; and greed or grievance debate 20-43; post-9/11 69; post-conflict needs assessment (PCNA) 79; and poverty reduction strategy papers (PRSP) 79; poverty reduction squeezed by development in complex conflicts 3, 115-16; as structural violence 24, 80
Pratt, Nicola 111
Protect, Respect and Remedy (guidelines) 35

provincial reconstruction teams (PRTs) 129
public service delivery 7, 18, 35, 37, 39, 52, 55, 56, 78-9, 99, 107, 120-1, 123, 124 , 128, 133
Putzel, J. 116

reconciliation processes 1, 81, 92, 127
reconstruction 4, 66, 94, 100, 123
refugees 1, 4, 40, 48, 49, 55, 92
Rehn, Elisabeth 103
resources for conflict analysis (*box*) 51-2
responsibility to protect 5, 35, 67, 70-1, 75, 128
Richmond, Oliver 117, 119, 133
Ruggie, John 35
rule of law 1, 4, 62, 72, 81, 120, 127, 128
Russia 40
Rwanda 4, 8, 25, 39, 69, 73, 85, 92, 98, 104, 105, 130

Saferworld 50, 51, 88
scapegoating 30
Scott, James 36
security and development 3-19, 33, 40-1, 48, 49, 50, 54-6, 66-9, 77-80; security–development nexus 80-1
security sector reform (SSR) 16, 55, 66, 68, 81, 83-4, 89, 90, 102, 127
security, community 83; human vs military 8, 63, 66-9, 77-80, 83, 90-1, 115-16, 163-4n
security, community-level 83;

environmental 84-6; and governance projects 81; underdevelopment as threat to 15, 72, 77, 116; women and 92-114

sexism 21, 24

sexual abuse and violence 9, 24, 56, 68, 69, 89, 92, 103-4, 107-113, 169n

Sierra Leone 34, 41, 48, 76, 105

Sjoberg, Laura 97-8

slavery 21

Smith, Anthony 26

social contract 78, 121, 128, 133

social justice 12, 14, 24, 64, 93

Somalia 4, 8, 9, 25, 40, 41, 69, 73, 87, 88, 126-7 (box)

sovereignty 7, 8, 49, 70-1, 73, 120, 127

Specht, I. 108

Srebrenica 69

Sri Lanka 8, 30, 39, 41, 109-10

state failure, *see* failed and fragile states

statebuilding 4, 7, 10, 18, 63, 77-80, 91, 99, 100, 101, 111, 113, 115-36

Stewart, Frances 38-9

strategic conflict assessment (SCA) 50

structuralism 11, 24

Sudan 6, 8, 9, 40, 41, 85, 107, 121, 130, 131

suicide bombers 94, 98

survival 22-3, 37, 46

Sweden 85

Swedish International Development Agency (SIDA) 51, 54

Sylvester, Christine 95-6, 102

Tamil Tigers (Liberation Tigers of Tamil Eelam) 109-10

Tanzania 85

terrorism 5, 18-19, 68-9, 73, 77, 135, 170n

Thailand 85

Timor-Leste 4, 9, 58, 59-60 (*box*), 74, 84, 105, 107, 121, 122-3 (*box*), 124-6

traditional structures 25, 26, 55, 120, 127-8

transitional administrations 4, 74, 121-3

trusteeship 25, 121, 164-5n

Uganda 6, 8, 85, 106, 130

Ul Haq, Mahbub 67

UN Action against Sexual Violence in Conflict (UN Action) 104

UNAMID 87

underdevelopment, as 'threat to security' 15, 72, 77, 116

United Nations (UN), and arms trade 82; Charter, Chapter VI 131-2; Congo operation (1960) 1; Department of Peacekeeping Operations (DPKO) 107; on gender and conflict 106; Human Rights Council 35; interaction with locals 117-18; Office for the Coordination of Humanitarian Affairs 129; Peacebuilding Commission 75-7; Secretary-General 1, 68, 104, 132; Security Council 3, 34, 71, 72, 75, 88, 103-4, 110-11, 128, 161n; Security Council Resolution (SCR) 1325 103–4,

105-7, 109, 111; Special Rapporteur on Human Rights 103; Special Representative on human rights and transnational corporations 35; Special Representative for Sexual Violence in Conflict 104, 106; Special Representative in Timor-Leste 121-3; and Timor-Leste 121-3; World Summit (2005) 68, 70, 76
United Nations Development Fund for Women (UNIFEM) 103-4, 106, 107
United Nations Development Programme (UNDP) 51, 54, 87

Vaux, Tony 50
Vietnam 85
violence, armed violence reduc-

tion (AVR) 82-3; culture of 56; domestic 83, 108; and employment 59-60 and human vs military security 66-9; masculinities and 102, 105, 107, 113-14; sexual and gender-based 9, 24, 56, 68, 69, 89, 92, 103-4, 107-13; structural 20-1, 22, 23-4, 42, 52, 64, 165n; urban 83, 105; youth 60-1, 63, 102, 105, 125

War on Terror 30, 77, 94, 111, 114, 116
water 46, 47, 49, 84-5
West Africa Network for Peace (WANEP) 88
West Bank 130
Wilson, E. O. 22-3
Women in Peacebuilding Programme (WIPNET) 106